The Visitor's Guide to
THE SOUTH OF FRANCE

FRANCE

Visitor's Guide Series

This series of guide books gives, in each volume, the details and facts needed to make the most of a holiday in one of the tourist areas of Britain and Europe. Not only does the text describe the countryside, villages, and towns of each region, but there is also valuable information on where to go and what there is to see. Each book includes, where appropriate, stately homes, gardens and museums to visit, nature trails, archaeological sites, sporting events, steam railways, cycling, walking, sailing, fishing, country parks, useful addresses — everything to make your visit more worthwhile.

Other titles already published or planned include:
The Lake District (revised edition)
The Peak District
The Chilterns
The Cotswolds
North Wales
The Yorkshire Dales
Cornwall
Devon
East Anglia
Somerset and Dorset
Guernsey, Alderney and Sark
The Scottish Borders
    and Edinburgh
The Welsh Borders
Historic Places of Wales
South and West Wales
The North York Moors,
    York and the Yorkshire Coast
Dordogne (France)
Brittany (France)
Black Forest (W Germany)

KEY FOR MAPS

▱ ●	Towns - Villages
⊖⁴	Motorways
▬	Main Roads
—·—·	Country Boundary
— —	County Boundary
⌒⌒	Rivers
⬭	Lakes/Reservoirs
⋔	Museum/Art Gallery/Centre
⏃	Archaeological Site
⊞	Building/ Country Park Gardens
☗	Castle/Fort
⋀	Ecclesiastical Building
❷	Wildlife Park/Zoo Nature Reserve
✳	Other Place of Interest

The Visitor's Guide To

THE SOUTH OF FRANCE

Norman Brangham

MOORLAND PUBLISHING

HUNTER
PUBLISHING INC

British Library Cataloguing in
Publication Data

Brangham, Norman
  The visitor's guide to the south of
  France.
  1. France, Southern — Description
  and travel — Guide-books
  I. Title
  914.4′804838   DC607.3

© Norman Brangham 1984

Published in the UK by
Moorland Publishing Co Ltd,
8 Station Street,
Ashbourne, Derbyshire,
DE6 1DE England.
Tel: (0335) 44486

ISBN 0 86190 112 6 (paperback)
ISBN 0 86190 113 4 (hardback)

Published in the USA by
Hunter Publishing Inc,
300 Raritan Center Parkway,
CN94, Edison, NJ 08818

ISBN 0 935161 21 X (paperback)

Printed in the UK by
Butler and Tanner Ltd,
Frome, Somerset.

ACKNOWLEDGEMENTS

I am indebted to the French
Government Tourist Office and Mrs
Florence Beddow for supplying some of
the colour transparencies and all the
black-and-white photographs which
illustrate this book.
  My thanks go also to Mrs Pauline
Hallam and Mrs Martine Williams at the
FGTO for their help in obtaining
material used in 'Further Information'.

The colour illustrations were supplied by:
The French Government Tourist Office
(Arles, La Ciotat), A.N. Brangham
(Eygalières), C. Macdonald (Port Cros,
Cavaliere, Port Grimaud), C.L.M. Porter (La
Napoule), R. Scholes (Montferrat, Verdon,
Col d'Allos, Monte Carlo).

Contents

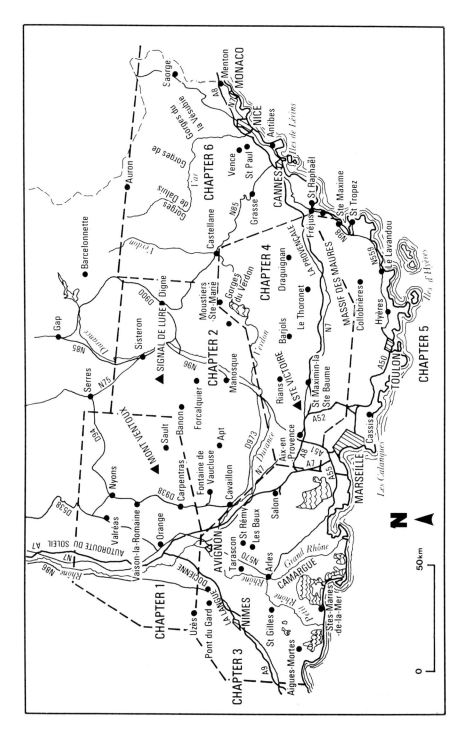

Introduction

What is the South of France?

For some people, the South of France is the whole French Mediterranean coast from the Italian to the Spanish frontiers. For most, it is the south-east corner of France which encompasses Provence and the Côte d'Azur, the region covered by this book.

Provence and Côte d'Azur: two names with enticing associations. Provence suggests vines, olives, herbs and sun-filled open landscapes and a profusion of antique monuments. The Côte d'Azur is synonymous with luxury set in semi-tropical splendour. These stereotyped ideas are not entirely accurate, as I shall show, but what is fact is that both areas belong to the Mediterranean's brilliant light and warmth, and Provence is geographically nearer to us than any other part of the Mediterranean Basin.

Where does the traveller from the north strike this Provence? The political map says that Provence and the Côte d'Azur are made up of five *départements*. Each equates, very roughly, with a British county, although the head of a *département*, the *préfet*, is a powerful political figure, appointed by central government and responsible to the Minister of the Interior. The five *départements* are, in the north, Vaucluse (taking in the east bank of the Rhône), and further east, the Alpes-de-Haute-Provence. South of these two are Bouches-du-Rhône, Var and Alpes-Maritimes, all of which border the sea.

I add the southern strip of a sixth, Drôme, where it fringes Vaucluse and happens totally to surround a lopped-off bit of Vaucluse. Southern Drôme is part of the old province of Dauphiné, but it is essentially Provençal. There are the same terracotta curled roof-tiles like skeins of unravelled orange and yellow wool; the same heavy-shadowed arcaded streets in clustered villages. Grignan, St Paul-Trois-Châteaux, Buis-les-Baronnies and Montbrun-les-Bains think of themselves as *la Dauphiné Provençale*. The major town, conscious of its touristic importance, proudly calls itself Nyons-la-Niçoise to emphasise — as do its olive groves — its climatic identity with the French Riviera.

Part of a seventh *département* must also be included. Just across the river Rhône is Gard whose Roman monuments link it to Provence.

From the Rhône, the natural frontier with Languedoc, to the Italian frontier is no more than 240km at the most; from Serre-Ponçon in the north of Alpes-de-Haute-Provence to the Iles d'Hyères, the southernmost islets off the Var mainland, is 160km. It is not a vast territory to encompass. Michelin maps (1cm to 2km) 84, 81 and a small eastern part of 83 cover the whole.

However often it is repeated, each entry into Provence seems to be different. This is not because some administrative boundary has been crossed which identifies it, but because the physical features become different. A climatic frontier is crossed. The vegetation changes; so does the quality of light. Some man-made things change, too, but nature gives the chief clue why

Provence, for all its Frenchness, is nonetheless a land apart. Deciduous trees give way to evergreens; in place of soft, springy turf is coarse, hummocky grass.

Provence obeys the rhythms of the Mediterranean climate. Seasons follow in abrupt succession. Sudden autumn rains end the panting heat of summer, and there are few autumn tints save among the vines and highland fruit trees and along river banks where poplars grow. Winters are mild, particularly along the sheltered parts of the coast.

Spring produces the year's most sustained rainfall. Dormant plant life explodes into growth and flowers and seeds before the rising heat of summer introduces a punishing drought which can last for three months. For the tourist these are the picture-postcard days when the scent of resin and herbs fills the air. Yet summer is when life is threatened by dehydration.

If I put on my naturalist's slouch-hat I like to say that Provence begins where anthills cease, but do not take this too literally. It illustrates that in the north nature harvests warmth and drains off excess moisture (which is what anthills do), while in the south living things ward off excessive warmth and aridity by searching for moisture in hidden crevices, cool and shaded north-facing slopes, and underground where water is stored.

Large areas of Provence lack water, though irrigation schemes have made much unproductive land fertile. Plants and animals which are not adapted to aridity do not survive. Even the non-naturalist can see how vegetation is

Olive trees, once venerated, their fruits still the basis of traditional Provençal cooking

dominated by somewhat dwarfed trees, as though to reach skyward would be injurious. Everywhere are evergreens which keep summer respiration to a minimum. A gentle sage-green colour paints the landscape all the year: holm and cork oaks; Aleppo, maritime and umbrella pines; and the quintessential symbol of the Mediterranean, the olive.

Where forests have been thinned, a *maquis* undergrowth of tree-heather, strawberry tree, juniper, myrtle, broom, cistus, butcher's broom, mastic and turpentine trees, makes a nearly impenetrable mass of rough and prickly shrubs.

Over wide clearings — and for thousands of years man has ruthlessly cut down forests for his many needs — rocks protrude like ribs out of the carcass of the land. This is the *garrigue*. In the thin soil grow the aromatic culinary herbs, low spiny shrubs such as kermes oak, gorse, ling, the myriad bulbs and tubers which flower briefly and profusely in spring to die back in the first parching weeks of summer, to leave a tawny desert.

What is common to these strange and attrative patterns of vegetation is the variety of ways which have been adopted to retain moisture and slow down its loss to the outer air. Trees have thick, roughened bark. Leaves are mostly small, sometimes reduced to mere thorns; leaves may be curled inwards, or they are thick, leathery or shiny; or else their undersides are covered with a down of pale hairs; many exude protective oils. The long, scimitar-shaped leaves of the eucalyptus turn so as to keep only the narrow edges of their blades facing the sun. Grasshoppers do the same. In Britain they place their flanks tilted full into the sun's rays (like basking blackbirds), while in Provence they face the sun head-on to ensure minimum exposure.

The climate is sometimes intemperate, and never more so than when the master-wind, the *mistral*, hurls itself down the funnel of the Rhône valley and imposes its will on western Provence. It is most violent in late winter and early spring when low atmospheric pressures over the Mediterranean Sea suck down air currents from the snow-covered Massif Central. A chill, insistent wind blows for a few days when temperatures can drop 10°C.

Observe how the old farmhouses (or *mas*) were constructed to withstand it. Squat and massive, the north side is often blank; windows are covered with hefty shutters which serve also to keep out the heat. Heavy roofs are weighted with rocks. Not that these defences make the interiors cosy; the *mistral* whistles through every cranny. Agriculturalists plant row on row of stately cypresses or bamboo as windbreaks for the tender crops.

Freezing and maddening the winter *mistral* may be — 'enough to pull the tail off a donkey' say the people of Avignon and Marseille which receive the fiercest lashings — but the purity of light it brings draws distant hills, almost invisible at other times, into startling detail. This is the time when the camera comes most effectively into its own.

Over the Rhône delta the wind fans east. The ranges of the Maures and Esterel break its power, and the Maritime Alps exhaust it to impotence. This fact, combined with the heat-storing and radiating rocks of the Côte d'Azur, is why Cannes, Nice, Monaco and Menton became pre-eminent as winter resorts.

Provence, to put it rather dramatically, is the most northerly perimeter of the Sahara desert. But for the almost tideless and strongly salted inland sea, Provence would be literally Saharan. The peerless summer is the hot air of tropical Sahara expanding northwards, diminishing from six months without rain in Algeria to three in Provence. Tropical air and polar air have their dogfights which produce the occasional but violent downpours of summer. Sometimes, hot gusts from Africa, the *sirocco*, carry clouds of sand-

Provence of contrasts: bulls in the watery flatlands of the Camargue

Provence of contrasts: arid hills round Beuil

particles, and the whole landscape is turned to an intense yellow or perhaps purple, according to how the sun's rays are refracted. In winter, the Saharan air retreats and cold continental air presses into Provence only to be heated by the warmth of the sea.

Average air temperatures show the general pattern of seasonal and geographical differences:

	Coast		Inland	
Jan/Feb	14 °C	56 °F	11 °C	52 °F
Mar/Apr	17 °C	62 °F	17 °C	62 °F
May/June	22 °C	72 °F	25 °C	77 °F
Jul/Aug	27 °C	81 °F	30 °C	86 °F
Sep/Oct	23 °C	73 °F	23 °C	73 °F
Nov/Dec	16 °C	60 °F	12 °C	53 °F

Countless distinguished writers have said how forcibly some part of Provence reminds them of this country or that from the four corners of the earth. Katherine Mansfield was reminded of her native New Zealand by the mountains behind Menton. Vincent van Gogh saw in La Crau round Arles a replica of his Netherlands homeland. The centenarian explorer, Alexandra David-Neel, living in the arid hills of Digne, felt she was almost in the Tibet she had got to know so well. Roy Campbell, the flamboyant rancher-poet, saw the Natal of his youth recreated in the Camargue. A corner in Var, when first I saw it, transported me with a shock to a familiar wartime stretch of the Algerian coast. The similarities are a form of flattery, but they show how much Provence is a landscape of many distinct characters. I call them *pays*. The word is hard to translate; 'country' or 'district' cannot convey the intimacy and rooted possessiveness implicit in its French meaning. Stemming from the Latin *pagus*, it carries a flavour of Provence's human antiquity. The diversity of these *pays* throws into relief innumerable contrasts within Provence,

11

Early spring is tree-frog belching time, part of the natural sound-rhythms of the year.

making it an endlessly rich region to explore.

How totally different is the cool pyramidal hump of chalk-dusted Mont Ventoux, 'the giant of Provence', across whose flanks float diaphanous purple and green shadows, from the buckled, seemingly molten ridges of Montagne Ste Victoire further south.

There are the paradoxical and mysterious wetlands of the Camargue whose flat horizons and bleaching light confuse sky, sea, lagoons and spits of land, whose southern tip is one of the most rainless areas of Provence.

Diversity is stamped on the coastline, too. The Maritime Alps behind the Côte d'Azur here and there threaten to hurl everything into the sea, so steep are the mountains. An exotic summer heat throws heavy and voluptuous shadows. To the west, the hills stand back, and the sands of Var radiate a clearer light in a drier atmosphere. Outside Cassis stands France's tallest coastal cliff. Outside Les Stes Maries-de-la-Mer the sands are backed by nothing higher than dunes, and Mont Ventoux, 100km away is a distinct blue convexity on the far horizon.

In Vaucluse, the yellow soil suffuses the buildings of whole villages; round Aix, the intense iron-oxide soil glows a vivid crimson-brown, especially after rain.

Olive trees in one district hardly look to be the same species as those in another. In the Rhône valley they are mostly pruned low and round. Behind Menton they are left to grow to full majestic height, groves of soft-shadowed grace.

If the countryside south of St Rémy is reminiscent of Virgil's Italy, the north slopes of La Ste Baume grow forests of beech, lime, maple, holly, all northern refugees from the last Ice Age stranded in the Mediterranean.

A mournful solitariness pervades the forested range of the Maures, while the Plateau de Valensole above the left bank of the river Durance emanates a vaulting thin light over the soft, undulating fields of lavender.

Note the contrast between the two great rivers of Provence. The broad Rhône is a fast-flowing frontier river, industrialised, impersonal. Its tributary, the Durance, once a seasonally destructive torrent, now tamed by dams, is still the true artery of Provence, as its silvery coils snake sluggishly past gravel-islets along a broad and smiling valley.

The rich variety of scenery means that

Papal chamber, Palace of the Popes, Avignon: part of a rich artistic inheritance

a diversity of habitats makes the whole country of absorbing interest to naturalists who come to Provence, much as medieval monks used to travel to it from all over Europe to gather herbs and simples.

Europe's richest concentration of avifauna is in the Camargue which has had more than enough exposure on television screens. Millions of birds migrate across Provence, though they rarely catch the casual eye. Dawn choruses are uncommon; you have to adjust to different seasonal sound-cycles. Instead of waking to the songs of garden and woodland birds, your sleep is broken into by choirs of nightingales in the thickets. Early spring is tree-frog belching time. In high summer the cicada's sizzling song splits the hot

Marineland, near Antibes

daylight hours. Late spring and autumn days and nights tremble to the melodies of crickets.

Zoologists can study beavers, boars, tortoises, reptiles, snakes (fortunately there are no adders below 1,000m!) and batracians. For botanists, hundreds of unfamiliar species and plant communities await identification in that diversity of habitats at which this chapter has already hinted. An arctic flora clings to the upper slopes of Mont Ventoux, a Mediterranean at its feet.

The serious horticulturalist will want to make his own arrangements to visit some of the private and public gardens on the Côte d'Azur where exotic trees and plants from all the continents have been acclimatised.

As readers of J.H. Fabre will know, Provence is fascinating for entomologists. But please refrain from cabinet collecting. Butterflies and moths appear in profusion, but the survival of some species is precarious. Observation of habits is pleasure enough. Large and showy insects attract the attention of every visitor: praying mantises, carpenter bees, locusts, scarab and capricorn beetles, emperor moths, swallowtail butterflies, and the ethereal silent tracer-lights of fireflies — the list is almost endless.

Nature is one magnet. Architecture and art of different epochs is the other. The celebrated monuments to the stonemason's craft, the creative vision of the artist, are achievements to which people travel from afar to admire: the relics of prehistory, the plethora of Roman monuments which are among the finest the Roman world has to show, medieval churches, Renaissance mansions, the art museums which make plain the long obsession of the artist with Provence, the striking new coastal architecture, and industrial complexes which challenge realism and sentiment.

Off the beaten track are half-forgotten ruins, wayside shrines and Romanesque chapels. They are like animals become half wild. To stumble across them, unaided by a guide book, is the wanderer's delight, clearly remembered when better-known images have receded.

Like the contrasts in nature, the obvious and the obscure among human artefacts together help complete an understanding of Provence. There is certainly something for everyone to enjoy and discover in all these Provences.

Chapters 1 to 6 are descriptions which cover the six areas of Provence and the Côte d'Azur. To keep them brief, only the more important sites and events of interest and entertainment are mentioned. Consult the extended (though not exhaustive) list of such centres placed in alphabetical order in the Further Information under the sections 'Outdoor Centres of Interest and Entertainment'; 'Annual Events'; 'Museums, Art Galleries and Buildings open to the Public'.

Pleasures of Touring

If Provence's natural environment is in striking contrast to central and northern France, the immediately practical aspects of touring in Provence share the same advantages with the rest of the country: roads and leisure facilities.

There are enough roadways into Provence to satisfy the most avid appetite for variety. It can be approached over the high Alps, through wide or narrow valleys, by straight roads across the plains, by riverside and seaside routes, from autoroutes to deserted lanes.

The network of roads allows quite remote hamlets to be reached by car. On the Michelin maps main roads are shown in red, direct link roads in yellow, and a maze of minor and often meandering roads with no colour at all. All categories of roads are usually well surfaced, cambered and maintained. Those of lesser importance may have only sketchy signposting, but these are the roads for map-reading dawdlers. It is easier to pull the car off them for the picnic or rest. True, petrol-pumps are fewer; nor do they have the roadside emergency telephones and services of the Touring Club de France which serve the main roads. But nowadays public callboxes are prominent in every village should it be found necessary to call for help or book a room for the night.

Country garage mechanics can rarely resist a challenge. The *mécanicien* may start by grumpily shrugging his shoulders and say he has more than enough work on his hands or that he knocks off in half-an-hour. Touch his pride. Ask him where, as he can't do it, the nearest garage is which will. Nettled by the innuendo, he will, like as not, give undivided attention and skill to what has to be done, whatever the time may be.

Leisure facilities in the way of amusement and entertainment for the whole family are provided by all towns and villages which are centres of tourism. Municipal swimming-pools, tennis courts, riding ranches, amusement parks, archery clubs, and mini-golf are widespread; places with natural advantages exploit them, such as water-sport amenities on artificial lakes. In every village square is a free drama-

Pottery making at Vallauris

Fruit, vegetable and flower markets add life and colour to towns and villages

show — the locals playing the 'national' game of Provence, *pétanque;* it is like bowls but accompanied by a rich assortment of gesture and well-turned expletives. This is a delightful spectator sport indulged in by arena-conscious participants. The same is true of bullfights in which a *cocarde* has to be planted between the bull's horns.

18-hole golf courses lie closer to the more sophisticated areas near the coast at Biot, Mandelieu, Mougins, Valbonne, Mont Agel in Alpes-Maritimes; Valcros, Valescure in Var; and Les Milles near Aix in Bouches-du-Rhône.

Every activity connected with the sea is available at coastal resorts, large and small, including thalassotherapy or sea-water treatment at St Raphaël.

There are clubs for nudists and speleologists, archaeologists and climbers. Nine of the larger towns have gaming casinos.

Summer courses on a wide spectrum of subjects, for both artist and artisan, are held in many villages which also sell local craft produce: pottery, carved olive-wood, jewellery, glassware, and fabrics. The most famous centre of all is Vallauris, whose pottery works were at one time greatly stimulated by Picasso's presence there. Such items make attractive presents to bring home.

Open-air markets supply the requirements of self-catering holidaymakers as well as the needs of the picnic basket. At the stalls are colourful and animated displays of fruit, vegetables, cheese, meat, fish, as well as clothes, materials, toys and kitchen utensils.

Religious, folkloric or cultural

festivals are held in towns and villages up and down the province at various times of the year; visitors can certainly watch them and in some instances join in.

For those who are active and can take a break during winter months the Provençal winter-sports resorts make a special appeal. Most are small compared with many in the Alps; some are long-established, while one, Isola 2000, is comparatively new. Snowfalls from December on are substantial while the daytime usually offers brilliant sunshine. Pra-Loup, Auron and Valberg-Beuil are the oldest resorts. La Foux-Allos, Le Sauze and Super-Sauze, all outside Barcelonnette, are newer, while Isola 2000 is, as its name indicates, the highest at over 2,000m. These ski-resorts are at no great distance by car from Nice.

Much on-the-spot information about attractions and special events can be gleaned from hotel proprietors, while local tourist offices are also helpful with leaflets and detailed guidebooks.

Tourist hotels are classified officially by the government in 'star' categories which range from ****L (the luxury 'palaces'), through three intermediate grades, to * which is of moderate, but quite adequate, comfort. These are objective ratings based on facilities in relation to the number of bedrooms; they are not in themselves recommendations of quality.

Many other, more modest, non-tourist hotels exist in most towns and villages. There are furnished rooms and flats to let. Properly equipped country houses, villas, cottages and farms (or self-contained parts of them) can be rented as a holiday home (*gîte rural*). Well-equipped camp and caravan sites, sometimes in very lovely settings, can be found everywhere between sea and mountains.

In July and August is the hot high season when it is improvident not to have booked holiday accommodation in advance. Even earlier and later in the season hotels in popular centres by the sea and inland tend to be fully booked. Particularly is this so in September when the stored warmth of late summer attracts many visitors.

The fabled 'palace' hotels of the Côte d'Azur, and the elegant and often beautiful *'Relais et Châteaux'* (there are twenty-four of them in our region) are real enough. Luxury can be bought at a price, but I assume most readers will be looking for those one- and two-star hotels which are reasonable as to both price and comfort. They may not have the cosy armchair comfort we often expect from hotels; traditionally, the French have not been interested in comfort, though things are changing. Wall-to-wall carpeting, divan beds, toile wallpapers, decorated tiles around the private bath, dainty lampshades and better lighting are becoming more in vogue as middle-class hoteliers enter the trade and bring aesthetic touches to a once more utilitarian occupation.

One- and two-star hotels make up most of the largest hotel-chain, the *Fédération Nationale des Logis et Auberges de France – Logis de France* for short. This is a loose and fundamentally independent association of nearly 4,600 hotels. All undertake to provide a good standard of welcome, comfort, cleanliness and food at reasonable, inclusive prices. They are small and medium-sized (many have less than twelve bedrooms) family hotels in rural areas and small towns. *Auberges* are smaller and simpler than *Logis* and so tend to be cheaper. There is no sacrifice of individuality on account of belonging to a chain.

At the time of writing, the *Logis* and

L'Oustaoù de Baumanière, Les Baux, one of the most famous hotel-restaurants in the world

Auberges are scattered about the *départements*: twenty in southern Drôme; thirty-nine in Vaucluse; twenty-two in Alpes-de-Haute-Provence; thirty-six in Bouches-du-Rhône; twenty-eight in Var; seventy in Alpes-Maritimes; and ten in eastern Gard. The annual handbook of these useful hotels is free to callers at the French Government Tourist Office, 178 Piccadilly, London W1. Some of them are included in the list of personally recommended small, W1 or from the French Government Tourist Office, 610 5th Avenue, New York. Some of them are included in the list of personally recommended small, reasonably priced hotels in the Further Information.

To paint a picture of what an authentic Provençal hotel is like means piecing together a composite picture, since they are all so very different. Perhaps the shell of the hotel is an eighteenth-century town house, grave and restrained to look at from the outside. The interior retains the old high-ceilinged beams. Polished walnut furniture with ornately moulded baroque panels are the bedroom wardrobes. On the bed is a cover of strong yellow, green or red, dotted with contrasting motifs of such charm as to make you want to go out and buy one at once. With luck, the bed-linen will be rough and white and lavender-sweetened. Copper pots hang on the restaurant walls. Each table is laid, a blaze of welcoming colour from the tablecloth to the rest of the napery and the polished glasses. The floor is surfaced with hexagonal terracotta tiles.

Of course, such hotels as the one I have reconstructed, emanating an atmosphere of yesteryear are less easy to find now that purpose-built hotels are going up in newly developed tourist areas.

Restaurants, like hotels, run the

gamut from the magnificent to the simple. Some of the most prestigious restaurants of the world are sited in our territory. Gastronomes come from far and wide to l'Oustaù de Baumaniére at Les Baux; to La Bonne Auberge at Antibes; Le Moulin de Mougins at Notre Dame-de-Vie outside Mougins; and l'Oasis at La Napoule, to name only those to whom experts have given the highest accolades. A meal at any of them is an experience; one does not quibble about cost.

Most visitors, looking for a more modest experience yet still memorable, turn to the annual Michelin red guide's maps of restaurants which provide 'good food at moderate prices'. Over the years I have found these recommendations reliable.

An even better source of information can be the place where one is staying. Fall into conversation with a French family familiar with the vicinity, and sage advice as to where the food is choice and the price right will be forthcoming.

Substantial and inexpensive meals are provided by *Les Relais Routiers*, sited mostly on main roads and catering orginally for lorry-drivers. Now passing motorists patronise them as well. At some, the surroundings are stark.

From time to time, at least, the visitor wants a genuine Provençal dish. The classic ones are expensive because of the materials required and the time they take to prepare. Happily, some dishes are not outrageously costly, and they should be looked out for.

Traditional Provençal food is distinctive, based on olive oil, herbs and garlic — 'the truffle of Provence' (and there are very good real truffles, too, from Vaucluse).

At this point, let me say to those who grimace at the mention of garlic that,

properly cooked garlic in Provençal dishes leaves no unpleasant smell or taste. It enhances the flavour of the dish. Raw garlic being chewed is the offender.

The menu which is displayed outside the door includes a fixed-price tourist menu, usually a basic, inexpensive three-course meal. A second *table d'hôte* will have more choice. A third, a *menu gastronomique*, including regional specialities, will also be shown. All the dishes appear on an *à la carte* list. It is almost invariably cheaper to choose the *table d'hôte*.

Consult one of the excellent books in English on regional French cooking before going to Provence so as to be alert to local specialities, of which only some can be mentioned here.

Near the coast fish and seafood dishes naturally take pride of place, and *bouillabaisse* is the classic dish. Experts disagree as to its vital ingredients, but basically it is a stew of a variety of Mediterranean fish, garlic and saffron. It must be ordered the day before and must be consumed with gusto and ritual by a party of four or more. Like some other great Provençal dishes, it is not for the budget- or calorie-conscious traveller.

The second great dish is *bourride*. Again, it is a stew, made with grey mullet, sea-bass, whiting and other white fish, topped with an unctuous mayonnaise of garlic and olive oil, *aïoli*, 'the butter of Provence'. *Aïoli* transforms plates of plain vegetables or hard-boiled eggs into a feast.

Every restaurant serves *soupe de poisson*. It can be something mediocre out of a tin or packet; at its best it is a stock of various fish, pungent and peppery, served with toasted cubes of bread, cheese and a rust-coloured sauce of garlic, hot peppers and saffron called *rouille* (which also means rust in French).

Brandade de morue is pounded dried salt cod made creamy with olive oil and milk; if it is on the menu at all it is likely to be on a Friday. Other sea fish which are seen on the slabs at market or in restaurants are John Dorey (*daurade*), sea-bass (*loup de mer*) and red mullet (*rouget*).

Nice, on account of its long political association until 1860 with Italy, has a distinctive, Italianate cuisine. Look out for *soupe au pistou*, a vegetable soup thickened with a *pommade* of pounded basil, garlic and olive oil. For a substantial picnic buy a *pan bagna*, French bread with olive oil, spread with chopped anchovies, tomatoes, onions and peppers. An alternative is *tourte aux blettes*, an open-crust pastry covered with leaves of chard (rather like spinach). Or else there is the local vegetable flan called *tian*. Or yet again, *anchoïade*, an open sandwich, hot or cold, with anchovy paste and oil, garlic and vinegar. Three Niçois names are known everywhere: *pissaladière* (akin to the Italian *pizza*), and *salade niçoise*.

The Camargue supplies the cattle for *boeuf en daube* stew in red wine and aromatic herbs, as well as *boeuf gardianne*. Rice-growing, now producing the lion's share of French rice consumption, gives a local risotto dish, *riz de Camargue*, of mussels and other sea-foods. Eels are bred in vast numbers in the Camargue; a local dish is of them stewed in wine and served with tomatoes and potatoes.

From the herb-covered hills comes succulent lamb, the small grey snails called *cantareu* in Provençal, rabbit, thrush and blackbird pâtés, and sometimes wild boar.

A splendid variety of early vegetables makes salads and *crudités* (raw vegetables which when attractively dressed and presented are a much-appreciated first course since the quantity of cooked vegetables with the main course is sometimes small). Tomatoes, cabbages, marrows, lettuce, dandelions, aubergines, pumpkin, artichokes, asparagus, pimentoes stuffed or combined in a variety of ways ought to avoid any complaint of repetitious meals.

The fresh fruits of Provence are famous: olives, figs, cherries, peaches, apricots, grapes, melons, as well as the ubiquitous golden and red delicious apples. Try the thirst-quenching *pastèque à la provençale*: chilled watermelon filled with either a fine red or rosé Provençal wine. Fritters made with flowers such as mimosa or marrow make agreeable sweet courses.

Cheese boards may be loaded with a variety of French cheeses, but those from Provence will be few, though the disc-shaped Banon goat cheese should be among them. Its flavour is delicate yet distinct, for it is first wrapped in the leaves of the herb savory, then dipped in *eau-de-vie* before receiving its final wrapping of vine or chestnut leaves and tied with straw. Allied to Banon is *poivre d'âne* or ass's pepper (*pebré d'assé* in Provençal), its peppery flavour imparted by finely ground savory leaves on the outside. Look out for the unusual strong ewe's milk cheese, *cachat*, in season between May and November.

For the sweet tooth the delicately almond flavoured *calisson d'Aix* biscuits are a temptation. Crystallised fruits of Apt; Spanish chestnut purée and *marron glacé* from Collobriéres; candied flowers and figs from Grasse and Nice; caramel sweets called *berlingots* from Carpentras (with a more fragile flavour than our boiled sweets); the famous nougat of Montélimar, whose ingredients are the high quality regional honey and almonds; nougat is also made in smaller

quantities at Draguignan, Sault and Sisteron.

Finally, the wines. For the most part, wines produced in the broad coastal belt of southern Provence have no great merit beyond, perhaps, their high alcohol content. These are the Côtes de Provence, Coteaux d'Aix and Coteaux du Var. Quantity rather than quality is the rule, but the reds go well enough with the robust meat dishes of Provence, and the whites and rosés adequately accompany fish.

Exceptions are the strong red and white wines of Bandol; the very dry Cassis white; Palette from near Aix produces red, white and rosé, of which the red from Château Simone is most highly regarded; Château Vignelaure, its

neat vineyards curving up at a bend in D561 between Rians and Jouques, produces a respectable red; Bellet, behind Nice, also makes a red, white and rosé wine in small quantities — it is a chic drink.

More interesting wines are found further afield. Stray into Gard to taste Tavel, the best dry rosé of all, at Tavel. Its near neighbour Lirac also produces a distinguished rosé. Near Aigues-Mortes is the 'wine of the sands', Listel *gris-de-gris* rosé.

Also in Gard, some 16km southwest of Nîmes is the Perrier factory. The famous mineral water rises as a spring from a subterranean lake and the fizzy soda-water is bottled under pressure. The plant can be visited most weekdays of the year.

Cross to the north bank of the Durance and you are in Vaucluse, the southern part of Côtes du Rhône country. Châteauneuf-du-Pape is the only classic wine of Provence, of which a little white is also produced. Gigondas is a good red from the slopes a few kilometres northwest of Châteauneuf.

When Côtes du Rhône labels are hyphenated with one of a dozen communes in Vaucluse, a bold, smooth wine is promised. A lighthearted, faintly sparkling rosé is Visan which gives a brief, champagne-like lift. Coteaux du Tricastin, Côtes du Luberon and Côtes du Ventoux have been imported into Britain for a number of years, during which time their quality has improved.

In Drôme is made a sparkling wine by the *méthode champenoise*, Clairette de Die, which comes both *brut* and *demi-sec*.

One of the lightest fortified sweet wines is Beaumes-de-Venise, drunk either as an aperitif or as a desert, as is its close neighbour, Rasteau.

The most popular of aperitifs — indeed the 'national' drink of Provence — is aniseed-flavoured *pastis*, clear until water is added, tasting innocuous to begin with; the kick comes a little later. A bar's shelf displays a bewildering variety of *pastis* bottles; it take constant practice for the taste-buds to distinguish them all. The indigenous variety is Ricard (a name associated all over Provence, not only with this drink but with Paul Ricard's leisure and sports centres as well). Recently, a non-alcoholic Ricard *pastis*, thick and sweet, has been put on the market. The other locally made aperitif is the quinine-based St Raphaël; the red is full and sweet, the white is drier and less fruity.

Something of a rarity is a yellow, pungent, herb-flavoured liqueur called Sénancole, originally developed (to a secret formula as these liqueurs always are) by the monks of the abbey of Sénanque, not far from the village of Gordes in Vaucluse.

Wine-tasting and comparing wine-notes are part of the delights of a holiday, but the truth has to be told that wine prices in restaurants are sometimes as high as they are in Britain. A local wine is not necessarily cheap for being local. Some restauranteurs still include a carafe of wine in the price of the meal; in Michelin this is indicated by the letters 'bc' (*boisson compris*) following the price of the meal. Others provide an acceptably priced carafe or jug (*pichet*) of *vin de table* or *vin du patron*.

Wine in groceries or supermarkets is still cheap. So it is at wine co-operatives, the *caves cooperatives* or *vinicoles*, which are dotted about the wine-growing districts.

A small *bonbonne*, a glass demi-john encased in whicker, holds 10 litres; the more practical *cubitaine*, the now familiar wine-box, is sold in various capacities from 10 litres to 33 litres. Wines which have been enjoyed on holiday can be bought in this way and stowed in the boot of the car. Even after duty has been paid at British customs, the purchase is worth while, all the more so if the quality of the wine is good, for the tax remains the same.

History in Brief

The last Ice Age had little direct effect on Provence; the glaciers retreated from further north. Conditions were favourable for a species of man from Africa to cross the Straits of Gibraltar and filter along the coast eastwards to reach the French Riviera a million years ago.

More definite evidence of human activity in Nice some 300,000 years ago came to light when rock-shelters were excavated. Early man fashioned a kind of ridge-tent from lashed branches and leaves which was a temporary shelter during seasonal migrations.

For tens of thousands of years man hunted, gathered and fished. Skeletons dated to 30,000BC, uncovered in the coastal Rochers Rouges outside Menton, were adorned with shell and fishbone necklaces and bracelets.

Burial-places of Stone Age man exist all over Provence, but cave-paintings which occur frequently in western France are conspicuously absent. The terrain of southern Provence was too rough and the climate too warm to support the great mammals — bison, mammoth, woolly elephant, reindeer — which were hunted and immortalised in paint by Upper Palaeolithic cave-artists in Dordogne. Ibex, red deer and rabbits were the staple meats of Provence, hardly heroic subjects to inspire masterpieces in cave-sanctuaries.

Quite suddenly hunting gave way to a pastoral life around 6,000BC. In south-west Provence wild animals were first domesticated in western Europe, a precocious Neolithic revolution which started a pastoral tradition which has been at the root of Provençal culture ever since, until industrialism supplanted it. Even in the last twenty years, this immemorial tradition was expressed by the *transhumance*, a slow, ritualised month's trek on foot by thousands of sheep and their escorts. They left the lowland pastures as late spring begins to shrivel the grass; they wound their way to the lower Alps and returned as the first snows fall in October. Recent laws have put an end to the tradition. Flocks were then carried by train; now lorries transport them, but the numbers involved have gradually dwindled.

On the stony plateaux round Bonnieux and Gordes are beehive huts or *bories*. Most are of relatively recent construction, but they are examples of how Neolithic man devised the first free-standing stone buildings. They were the work of the early semi-nomadic shepherds who had been driven to the plateaux by farmers settled on the richer lower ground.

46,000 rock-carvings in the Val des Merveilles above Tende are adduced as evidence of Bronze Age shepherds who came each summer to these inhospitable highland valleys, although the meaning of the petroglyphs remains enigmatic.

All these early semi-nomadic shepherds, along with traders in skins and salt, trod out the first recognisable tracks which became the waymarks for Roman engineers later to construct the stone-slabbed highways.

Until the coming of the Romans, Provence north of the Durance was occupied by Celtic tribes; south of it by the Ligurians. Some of their dolmens still stand. *La Pierre de la fée* outside Draguignan is the most impressive. They built the first *oppida*, defensive positions of drystone walls at vantage points. Their residual heaps of stones can still be found on some hilltops, the one at Chastelard-de-Lardiers in the Lure mountains was also a major religious sanctuary. Examples of strange Celto-Ligurian art are in museums at Marseille, Aix and Avignon.

Traders from the eastern Mediterranean had been sailing along the Provençal coast from at least 1,000BC, until in 600BC Phoenician navigators founded a Greek colony on the site of Marseille, which they called *Massalia*. They traded with the natives, introduced the vine and the olive, founded trading posts east and west along the coast, and pacifically

Fontanalba Valley, close to prehistoric rock-engravings of Val des Merveilles

penetrated the Rhône valley. The Greek foundations of *Massalia* have been laid bare; Greek buildings can be seen at the open-air site of Glanon outside St Rémy; the Greek defensive wall at St Blaise is still in mint condition.

As Marseille expanded, its commercial power clashed with the interests of the Carthaginians and Etruscans. It was natural for Marseille to side with the Romans when the Punic Wars broke out. The Celts allied themselves with Carthage and, well bribed by Hannibal, gave him and his elephants passage along the Rhône and into the Alps for his attack on Rome in 218BC.

When Rome acquired provinces in Spain, Marseille assisted by keeping open the land route through Provence and subscribing a fleet which hastened the Carthaginian defeat at sea.

Antibes and Nice, outposts of Marseille, came under threat in 181BC from pirates. Rome came to the rescue, and Marseille found itself relying more and more on Rome's military might. By 125BC Rome had largely subjugated the

Roman Trophy of the Alps, La Turbie, commemorating the subjugation of the tribes in the Maritime Alps

lands between the Alps and the Pyrenees. Marseille became Roman; its name was changed to *Massilia*. Roman garrisons were installed; a huge *Provincia Romana* was created, of which today's Provence is only a fragment.

The strategic highways were built, of which traces can still be seen. *Via Aurelia* was the main artery between Rome and Spain, following the Italian coast to Nice and Fréjus, then inland through Le Luc, Aix, Salon and Nîmes, essentially the same route that the RN7 takes now. The demi-god Hercules was supposed to have walked this way on his return from the Garden of the Hesperides, and Monaco was named after him, *Portus Herculis Monoeci*.

Via Domitia descended the mountains by way of Embrun, Sisteron and Apt to join *Via Aurelia*, while *Via Agrippa* led north from Arles to Avignon, Orange and St Paul-Trois-Châteaux. Numerous branch roads gave an effective network of communications.

As southern France became Romanised there were tribal disputes, revolts against bureaucracy, taxation and commercial exploitation, but Julius Caesar was to govern the region for seven years with skill and authority. With the decline in the power of Marseille — hastened by its mistaken support of Pompey in his struggle with Caesar — Arles inherited supremacy.

Provence can be said to have prospered under Roman rule, particularly during the reign of

St Trophime, Arles, built on the pilgrimage route to St James of Compostela, Spain

Augustus when agriculture, stock-breeding and trade expanded. Arles became the granary of Rome. Goods were transported across the sea by the powerful guilds of boatmen (*utriculariae*, because they kept their cargoes afloat by means of inflated bladders) in the Rhône delta. Natives could become Roman citizens, and Roman law was tolerant of alien religions as long as Rome's absolute authority was not questioned. Christians, who first appeared in Marseille in AD95, did not acknowlege this authority and suffered persecution until Christianity was made the official religion by Constantine the Great, early in the fourth century. He himself settled in Arles, which was by then the second city of the Empire and known as 'the little Rome of the Gauls'.

The Romans gave to all France south of the river Loire the Low Latin occitan tongue of which Provençal is a derivative, a language used by all classes and the medium in which the

27

troubadours of the Middle Ages expressed their formalised love-songs.

Attracted by the wealth of Arles, the Visigoths in AD413 began the first of many sieges of it and of Marseille. Although they were unsuccessful they heralded the disintegration of the Western Roman Empire, leading to Provence coming under the rule of the Franks in 536. They left it as a semi-autonomous state.

When the Arabs crossed the Pyrenees they were not halted until Charles Martel defeated them at Poitiers in 732. To stop them crossing the Rhône, he invaded Provence which called on the Arabs for help. After seven years Martel had won, returning a sacked and massacred Provence to the firm administration of the Frankish Empire. The eighth century was one of the most tragic in Provençal history. Saracen raids continued from the sea and from their settlements near Hyères and St Tropez until their final defeat in 972.

Long periods of anarchical feuding, depopulation and pestilence ensured the economic and moral decline of Provence. But early in the thirteenth century the wise rule of Raymond-Berenger V unified and modernised the country and gave it a sense of identity.

Intrigue and marriage gave Provence in 1246 to Charles of Anjou who became Charles I of Provence and King of Sicily, an act of inheritance which the port of Marseille turned to great profit.

This was the period of the great religious pilgrimages which saw the building of splendid Romanesque churches such as St Trophime at Arles and at St Gilles, as well as many rural churches and chapels. St Louis set off on the Seventh Crusade from Aigues-Mortes in 1248. The art of the troubadours flourished at the Courts of Love, of which Les Baux was one of the most famous.

In 1229 the territory of Comtat Venaissin, which approximated to present-day Vaucluse (though excluding Avignon, Orange and some other bits of land) was bought for 80,000 florins by the Pope in Rome, and so it became detached from the rest of Provence. In the following century the Popes acquired more territories including Valréas (now a little enclave of Vaucluse surrounded by Drôme). They remained the possession of the Holy See until 1791.

Suddenly this corner of Provence, hitherto unimportant in the wider affairs of Europe, held the centre of the stage. In 1309, a French pope, Clement V, fled Rome, settled at Avignon, and installed the Holy See in what was to become the massive fortified Palace of the Popes. Five Popes ruled there until 1377, when the papal court returned to Rome. The Comtat Venaissin was henceforth administered by papal legates for more than 400 years.

In this phase of power and pomp, Avignon attracted the political, financial, intellectual and artistic elite of Europe. While the rest of Provence suffered incursions from Gascons, Spaniards, English, and the freebooters of Du Guesclin — all part of the devastating effects of the Hundred Years' War — the presence of the Popes ensured a measure of protection to the papal territories.

In the fifteenth century an economic and artistic upsurge came under the impetus of René d'Anjou, poet and artist with neither political nor military gifts. He is remembered as Good King René.

After his death in 1480, Provence (excluding the Comtat Venaissin and Monaco) entered into formal union with the crown of France. Royal power was exercised through the Parliament of Aix. Official transactions had now to be

Plaque in Cannes recalling Lord Brougham's stay in 1834 to start the long association between the British and Cannes

conducted in French, not Latin, to the resentment of many Provençaux who felt they were being deprived of their cultural heritage and identity by this centralisation. Resentment simmered until it found creative expression in the Provençal Renaissance of the nineteenth century under the authority of the poet Mistral.

In the mid-sixteenth century, the Luberon hills witnessed massacres and the total destruction of villages. The victims were the Vaudois, a fundamentalist heretical sect akin to the Albigensians in Languedoc who were dealt with cruelly early in the thirteenth century. All Protestant settlements in Provence provoked hostility with Catholics; the two sides became embroiled in the Wars of Religion

between 1560 and 1598 when the Edict of Nantes (revoked in 1685) was supposed to give freedom of worship and conscience. In fact, not until the Edict of Toleration in 1787 were Protestant minorities freed from the fear of persecution.

With the opening of the eighteenth century it looked as though stability and prosperity would return. Instead, Provence found itself devastated by the worst of many visitations of the plague. In 1720 a ship from the Levant brought it to Marseille. The main towns were decimated; 90,000 people died in two years. The authorities of the papal estates put up a wall, 100km long with sentry boxes every so often in the hope of confining the plague to the Provençal side. Traces of the wall can still be found

near Pouraque, south of Venasque. St
Sebastian transfixed by arrows, a
common pictorial theme in churches and
chapels, symbolically represented the
dreaded plague.

Yet, in the wake of distress, prosperity
did come. Merchants of Marseille and
Aix built their handsome *hôtels* or town
mansions, country seats, new churches
and public buildings, and Aix became a
centre of elegance and learning.

The Seven Years' War (1756-63) had
an unforeseen benevolent consequence.
Nice and its *Comté* belonged to the
Dukes of Savoy and the King of
Sardinia, allies with Britain in maritime
rivalry with France. British families

lived in Nice. Tobias Smollett, learning
of the delights of its climate, visited Nice
for his health in 1763-5, and wrote his
influential (and still very readable)
Travels. They marked the beginning of
the association of the British with the
Côte d'Azur; Lord Brougham, a century
later, discovered Cannes, and Dr Henry
Bennet, Menton.

A gradual convergence of social and
economic unrest throughout France —
flagrant inequalities; selfish and
absentee landlords; despotism;
corruption; mal-administration and
unfair taxation; high grain prices
particularly in Marseille and Toulon; a
grain failure after a cold winter — these

Giuseppe Garibaldi 1807-82 (Nice).
Italian general and patriot.

Honoré Daumier 1808-79 (Marseille).
Painter and penetrating political
caricaturist.

Frédéric Mistral 1830-1914
(Maillane).
Poet, leader of Provençal literary
revival.

Paul Cézanne 1839-1906 (Aix).
Neo-Impressionist profoundly
influencing European art.

Emile Zola 1840-1902 (Aix).
Novelist, boyhood friend of Cézanne.

Auguste Escoffier 1847-1935
(Villeneuve-Loubet).
Chef, inventor of *pêche Melba* at
Carlton Hotel, London.

Albert Calmette 1863-1933 (Nice).
Inventor of anti-tuberculosis vaccine.

Edmond Rostand 1868-1918
(Marseille).
Dramatist, poet, author of *Cyrano de
Bergerac.*

Raimu (Jules Muraire) 1883-1946
(Toulon).
Great Provençal screen character
actor.

Edouard Daladier 1884-1970
(Carpentras).
Radical politician, prime minister
1938-40.

Fernand Benoît 1892-1969 (Avignon).
Distinguished archaeologist.

Darius Milhaud 1892-1972
(Marseille).
Composer, member of 'Les Six'.

Jean Giono 1895-1970 (Manosque).
Major novelist using regional
landscapes as backgrounds.

Marcel Pagnol 1895-1974 (Aubagne).
Film-maker and writer.

Fernandel (Fernand Contandin)
1903-71 (Marseille).
Commic screen actor depicting Vieux
Port Marseillais.

factors precipitated the French
Revolution in 1789. In 1788, the
Parliament of Aix had protested against
the privileges and perquisites enjoyed by
the nobility and clergy. Passions were
inflamed in Provence by Count
Mirabeau, a powerful orator, through
his *Address to the Provençal Nation.*
Violence was widespread. The
Parliament of Aix held its last meeting
and with that ended the constitution of
Provence.

In 1789, the National Assembly in
Paris abolished the Aix parliament by
decree, and the administration of the
province was effected by three
départements, newly created: Bouches-
du-Rhône, Var and Basses-Alpes. Two
years later, during which there was
virtual civil war in the region, the
Comtat Venaissin was given up by the
Popes and became the fourth
département, Vaucluse. Nice and
Monaco temporarily joined the new
département of Alpes-Maritimes.

A contingent of volunteers marched
from Marseille to Paris in support of the
revolutionary cause. They brought with
them a new and rousing song which
came to be known as the 'Marsellaise'.

Broadly, the revolution was espoused
by the urban working classes in
Provence who were known as 'The
Reds'. Conservative rural communities

Modernity: terraces, gardens of Cannes' International Congress Centre, looking towards the Esterel Mountains

tended to have monarchical sympathies and were 'The Whites'. When the king was executed in 1793 there was widespread revulsion against the Revolution, and Toulon even opened its port to the young Republic's enemies, the Anglo-Spanish fleet.

The Convention in Paris sent an army to recapture Avignon and Marseille where 'The Whites' briefly dominated, and, after weeks of siege, Toulon, where one Captain Napoleon Bonaparte distinguished himself.

For all the great social and legal reforms introduced by Napoleon, his relations with Provence were not happy. Royalists felt affronted when he proclaimed himself Emperor. Commercial interests suffered as a result of the Allied blockade his campaigns brought about. On his way to the Elban exile the Provençaux threatened his life. When he landed at Golfe-Juan in 1815 for the 100 Days, the first part of his

journey towards Paris along stony tracks which approximate to the proudly named *Route Napoléon* (RN85) was that of a fugitive, abused and cheated, until the first cheers greeted him at Gap.

With the collapse of Napoleon's empire, royalists in Provence started a brief reign of 'white terror' by assassinating Bonapartists in Marseille and Avignon. From these events, and for fifty years afterwards, Parisians convinced themselves that the Provençaux were brutal reactionary fanatics.

The restoration of the Bourbon monarchy in 1814 led to the July Revolution of 1830, and the next king from the House of Orleans gave birth to the greater upheaval of 1848. Neither regime sensed the mood of the people and the growing ideas of socialism. The next king, Napoleon III, nephew of Bonaparte, was for a while popular in most of France, but not in Provence.

Provençal bullfighting at Arles

Chapelle St Sixte, Eygalières

Water-jousting at La Ciotat

Montferrat

Provence's most popular poet, Frédéric Mistral: statue in Arles, Place du Forum.
Fragment of Roman forum embedded in wall

Only after the ill-judged Franco-
Prussian war of 1870-1, when a new
republic was established, did the
government reflect the long-held

egalitarian and democratic traditions and the new-found patriotism of Provence.

New industrial technologies — metallurgical and chemical among others — came to Provence. Bridges were thrown across the Rhône and Durance; bauxite was first mined at Les Baux; railways, canal systems and marshland drainage were extended; steam navigation favoured the growth of Marseilles.

Agriculture, still the mainstay of Provençal life, suffered vicissitudes. Wheat, sheep and olives remained static staples, but the silkworm cottage industry was destroyed by disease; vineyards were ruined by phylloxera and their slow recovery was largely due to Pasteur's discoveries; the madder dye industry was quickly supplanted by German chemicals. Rural depopulation gathered pace as youth was drawn to the coast and to industry, and the Basses-Alpes became one of the poorest *départements* of France.

World War I left the territory of Provence untouched, but bled its manhood and bequeathed stagnation. World War II saw the Italians occupy the Côte d'Azur. The French fleet scuttled itself in Toulon. After 1942, the Germans occupied the whole of the Midi which was to know deprivation, deportation, the *maquis*, Allied air attacks, destruction by retreating German divisions, airborne and seaborne landings, liberation and recriminatory vendettas.

The Algerian War brought to Provence large numbers of French refugees who have been absorbed into the social, commercial and political life of the province. A whole town, Carnoux, was built for them. At different periods influxes of Italians, Spaniards and Algerians have supplied the unskilled and semi-skilled labour on roads, building sites and in vineyards.

Provence, whose existence as a political reality was erased by the Revolution, has been reborn officially, though its geography and political intention are different. In 1956 the central government created a series of economic regions in France. Provence was resurrected as Provence-Côte d'Azur-Corse: the five *departements* this book is about, plus Corsica and Hautes-Alpes, the latter an error of judgement for traditionalists.

Great changes have been wrought in thirty years. Now, only a small percentage of the population works on the land, but agricultural productivity has been vastly increased. Industry has tended to concentrate along the Rhône valley: petro-chemicals, electronics, hydro-electrics, iron, steel, aluminium, cement, nuclear fission for civil and military purposes, food production, and tourism.

The tourist may not be interested in this face of Provence, but it is a face of prosperity which has put Provence in the forefront, and no longer in the backwater, of European affairs.

1 The Rhône Valley to Avignon

The traditional highway from the north into Provence is the valley of the river Rhône. Until the railways came the produce of Provence was loaded on to great barges at Avignon and hauled by teams of horses to Lyon and beyond. Visitors came south by boats which had to shoot the twenty-five arches of the still standing medieval bridge at Pont St Esprit. A swift current demanded skill and sobriety of the pilot and steady nerves of his passengers.

Most now travel by the N7, some of whose traffic is absorbed by the *Autoroute du Soleil* (A7), while the west bank's N86 gets the motorist as rapidly into Provence as does N7 on the east bank.

A more rural route climbs out of Vienne and follows the edge of the Dauphiné foothills through Romans-sur-Isère, Crest, Nyons, Carpentras and to Cavaillon. As far as Nyons this is the D538.

Nyons is in Drôme, yet makes a good preparation for Provence proper.

Open-air museum in Vaison-la-Romaine: Empress Sabina

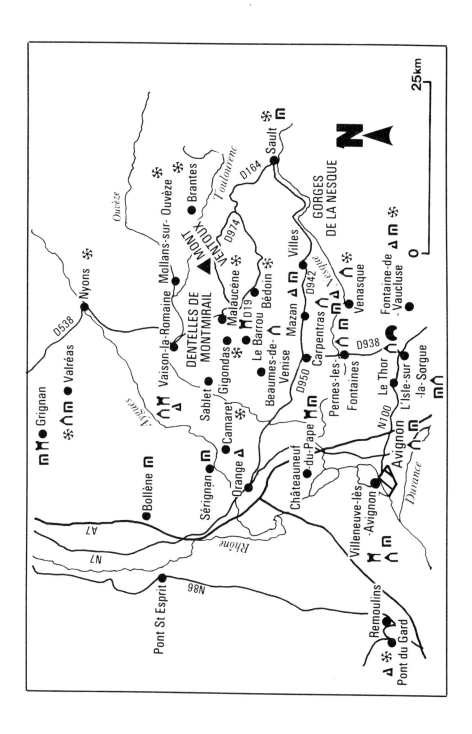

25km

N

Sault ✳ ▥

GORGES DE LA NESQUE

Toulourenc

D164

Brantes ✳

✳ Mollans-sur- Ouvèze

Ouvèze

MONT VENTOUX

D974

Fontaine-de ▲ ▥ ✳
-Vaucluse

Villes

Malaucène ✳

Bédoin ✳

Mazan ▲ ▥

Venasque ∩ ✳

Nyons ✳

D19

Le Barrou

D942

Nesque

Vaison-la-Romaine

DENTELLES DE MONTMIRAIL

Beaumes-de- ∩
Venise

Carpentras ∩ ∩ ▥ ▲

D538

Valréas ∩ ▥ ✳

Gigondas ✳

Pernes-les- ∩
Fontaines

D938

L'Isle-sur ▥ ∩
-la-Sorgue

Grignan ▥ ✵

Sablet

Camaret ▲ ✳

Beaumes-de-
Venise

D950

Le Thor

N100

Aygues

Châteauneuf
-du-Pape ✵ ▥

Avignon ∩ ▥

Bollène ▥

Sérignan

Orange ▲

Villeneuve-lès-
-Avignon ✵ ∩ ▥

Durance

A7

N7

Rhône

N86

Pont St Esprit

Remoulins ∩

Pont du Gard ▲ ✳

36

French families stay there in summer and winter, for the rounded, shrub-dotted hills shelter the resort from the *mistral*. In summer, the cooling *pontias* breeze blows down the valley of the Aygues (or Eygues or Aigues — all mean 'water'). Arcaded streets lead to medieval Nyons, the Quartier des Forts. Take the narrow road known as the *Promenade des Anglais* northwest out of Nyons for a circular trip to view the town and the valley.

West of Nyons is Valréas, chief town of the Vauclusian enclave surrounded by the Drôme *département*. Typical of so many towns (or *bourgs*) of Provence, Valréas stands on an eminence; its circular boulevards overhung with plane trees keep the old part intact.

Grignan, 9km to the north-west, is a place of literary pilgrimage for admirers of Madame de Sévigné, whose letters in the seventeenth century about court life in Paris and the Provençal countryside are still read. The château of Grignan (sixteenth century) stands out from afar.

The D538 south of Nyons enters Vaucluse at Vaison-la-Romaine. A hundred years ago, Baedeker did not mention the place, for the fame of Vaison began only with the excavation of Roman *Vasio* in 1907. A patrician city, it retained its reputation until the Franks destroyed it 400 years later.

Medieval and Roman Vaison are surrounded by the modern town on the right bank of the river Ouvèze. The one-time cathedral of Notre Dame de Nazareth (twelfth and thirteenth centuries) gives a good idea of the simple strength of Provençal Romanesque architecture. It stands on the site of a sixth-century church, parts of which are preserved in the structure of the later building.

To reach the Upper Town, a maze of old streets and houses, occasional

---

MAIN SIGHTS IN ROMAN VAISON

In Puymin Quarter
House of the Messii: inner courtyard, living rooms, library-room, kitchen, baths, latrine, mosaics.
Portico of Pompey: columns of public promenade, statues (reproductions).
Nyphaeum: source of town's water supply.
Theatre: reached by Roman tunnel, restored amphitheatre and rear colonnade.
Museum: statues, utensils, ceramics, coins excavated at Vaison.

In Villasse Quarter
Streets, pavements, arcaded shops, commercial basilica, public buildings, latrine with seats for five. House of the Silver Bust and House of the Dolphin.

---

fountains and a seventeenth-century chapel, cross the single-span Roman bridge over the Ouvèze. A ruined castle of the Counts of Toulouse, the feudal owners of the town, crowns the hill.

The prime excursion from Vaison is to the top of 'the giant of Provence', Mont Ventoux (1,912m). Choose a clear day, for the rounded white head of the mountain often wears a thick halo of cloud. The direct route is by Malaucène, its main streets massively guarded by plane trees. Clement V, the first of the Avignon popes, had the church built early in the fourteenth century, and Malaucène (the name means 'bad sands' on which it had been built) was his summer residence.

The D974 passes a delightful twelfth-century chapel — one of hundreds to be met with all over Provence — and then the source of the Groseau stream, harnessed by the Romans through a now vanished aqueduct.

It is 21km to the top of Ventoux, first through forest, then pasture and finally bare, stony slopes. If the day is clear it is likely to be windy; Ventoux means 'the Windy One', whose high point is called Col des Tempêtes. About the summit are a hotel, Ste Croix chapel, observatory, Air Force radar station, television masts and a plaque commemorating the climb undertaken by the poet Petrarch and his brother on 9 May, 1336, then an audacious assault in order to see the views — the first tourists.

The views are tremendous. From the viewing-table a panorama carries the eye from the sea beyond Marseille to the Pelvoux Massif in the northeast. With luck, Mont Canigou in the eastern Pyrenees can be seen. Dawn and dusk provide the most breathtaking moments, as Petrarch found.

Descend to Chalet Reynard; swing right through St Estève to Bedoin, a large village of ochre-coloured houses and little squares.

About 3km out of Bedoin, set back a little from D19 is the Chapel of Ste Madeleine, to my mind one of the most enchanting of rural chapels. The simple, square building is eleventh century, and is clearly derived from the Roman basilica. Bereft of ornament, it is gently severe. A sloping roof holds a square belfry, domed by a stone-tiled skull-cap, in place. A tiny slit aperture is at first floor level, a small rounded double aperture above, and highest of all, a proportionately larger double orifice. Three rounded apses, each crowned by Provençal tiles, cling like upside-down swallows' nests to the apsidal wall.

Views from the top of Mont Ventoux are spectacular, but there are even more satisfactory ways of savouring the majesty of it.

From Vaison make for Entrechaux and turn right just before Mollans-sur-Ouvèze. An east west road of some 25km keeps the north flank of Mont Ventoux in sight all the way. The road runs above the poplar-lined Toulourenc valley. Steep slopes rise sheer to the top, buttressed by huge pyramids of grey limestone, and yellow sandstone which seems to cement the whole bastion in place.

Turn left up the hill to see the precariously balanced village of Brantes. It commands an extended view of the bare, flat ridge of Ventoux. Good walkers can cross the Toulourenc stream and ascend the Ventoux by the marked GR9 track. In June, round Brantes, they gather lime blossoms which are dried and made into *tisane* herbal drinks.

Continue eastwards and turn right at Reilhanette, to Sault whose belvedere looks on to the sunbaked southern face of Ventoux. In July, great acres of lavender perfume the town.

From Sault to Carpentras is 45km by D942. A considerable length of the route is taken up by the gorges of the Nesque. From the first signposted belvedere can be seen the Rock of Wax (Le Rocher du Cire) where generations of wild bees have nested, coating the rock with wax. Frédéric Mistral, in his epic poem *Calendau* wrote of the Rocher du Cire, and the lines are quoted on the stele at the viewpoint.

At the end of the deeply incised gorge, the landscape opens out on to the Plain of Comtat Venaissin. At Villes-sur-Auzon another excursion can be made up the Combe de l'Hermitage which rejoins D942 near Sault, a narrow, winding but attractive route.

On the eastern outskirt of Mazan is a cemetery along whose retaining walls are ranged sixty-two Gallo-Roman sarcophagi, taken from the Carpentras to Sault roadside. The sarcophagi at Arles are more famous, but Mazan's can be inspected in tranquillity. Also in the Mazan cemetery is the half-buried chapel of Notre Dame de Pareloup (Our Lady Protectress against Wolves), first built in the twelfth century to exorcise demons in the guise of wolves which devoured buried corpses; wolves did prowl freely in these parts during cold winters.

Approaching Carpentras, a handsome aqueduct of forty-eight arches, 729m long and built between 1720 and 1729 to supply the town's water, appears on the right. Carpentras is a lively market-town of well over 25,000 inhabitants, ringed by boulevards, and lying in a fertile market-gardening plain. The town is sometimes called 'the crucible of Mont Ventoux', for the mountain watches over it.

Most of the interesting sights are in the narrow streets of the old town. Sightseeing is best done on foot. Park the car either near Place de Verdun or in Boulevard Maréchal Leclerc. Friday mornings are market days; there is a general market, a flea market, and a truffle market between late November and late March, for truffles are a pride of Vaucluse.

The only vestige of the ramparts put up by the Popes in Avignon in the fourteenth century is the Porte d'Orange, a 27m-high fortified and restored tower near where Boulevard Leclerc and Boulevard du Nord meet.

An eye-catching building in Place Aristide Briand is the elegant eighteenth-century hospital, the Hôtel-Dieu whose upper balustrades are surmounted by carved oriflammes. Inside is a graceful monumental stairway; the eighteenth-century pharmacy displays local and Italian faïence-ware behind painted cupboards.

The one-time Gothic cathedral of St Siffrein (the patron saint of Carpentras who appears in no orthodox hagiography, but may have been a sixth-century monk, Siffred or Siegfried, who came to evangelise the area), is entered by the south door. This is the Jews' Door by which Jews, recently converted to Christianity, went to worship.

Inside are figures by the sculptor Jacques Bernus (1650-1728) from Mazan, the greatest Provençal sculptor after Pierre Puget; and paintings by two artists whose works hang in innumerable churches and museums in Provence, Nicolas Mignard (1606-68), a Provençal by adoption, and Pierre Parrocal (1664-1739), one of a large family of Parrocel painters.

Next to St Siffrein is the seventeenth-century Palais de Justice or Law Courts whose court rooms are decorated with striking friezes. Behind is tucked the Roman Municipal Arch, erected in the first century AD during the reign of the Emperor Nero. It marked the entrance to the Gallo-Roman town, originally called *Carpentoracte* and changed to *Forum Neronis*. Although not well preserved, its bas-reliefs of two prisoners are distinct; they commemorate the victories of Augustus in Germany and the East.

A little to the north-east and reached by Rue d'Inguimbert is the oldest synagogue in France, although it has been much reconstructed. The first building was erected in 1367 when the Popes at Avignon were heavily dependent on Jewish financiers, and gave Jews sanctuary in Comtat Venaissin when they were expelled from France and the rest of Provence. Consequently, the town, like Cavaillon, had a flourishing Jewish ghetto. Baths for ritual purification, including one for women and called in Provençal the

*Notre Dame d'Aubune, Romanesque chapel with unusual belfry,
near Beaumes-de-Venise*

---

cabussadou ('head first'), are in the
basement. Ovens for baking unleavened
bread can be seen. Carved woodwork,
panellings, wrought ironwork,
candlesticks and other liturgical objects
impart an air of delicate elegance.

For the non-specialist the Comtadin

Museum in Boulevard Albin-Durand is
enjoyable. Objects in daily use years ago
make it an agreeable bygones collection.
Especially interesting are the bells used
for the age-old sheep-drives, the
transhumance, because Carpentras was
the centre where generations of bell-

makers named Simon worked. All the bells of different shapes and tones for sheep, rams, goats, donkeys and horses were made to harmonise musically as in a carillon, for the sheep-drive was conducted in a recognised order of procedure, almost as a religious ritual. So great was the Simons' reputation that the market-stalls in all Provence sold no other bells but theirs.

Above the Comtadin Museum is the Duplessis Museum of paintings by local artists, while local archaeology is displayed in the Lapidary Museum, Rue des Saintes-Maries.

The return to Vaison gives intriguing glimpses of the Dentelles de Montmirail which call for a separate excursion.

No doubt called by the Romans *Mons mirabilis*, the Dentelles de Montmirail is a small range of dramatic, naked rocks, elegantly eroded into a calcareous lacework, ideal for rock-climbing. They rise to a little over 730m but look higher, and are virtually encircled by the roads between Vaison, Malaucène, Beaumes-de-Venise, and Sablet.

Leave Vaison by D938 and just before Malaucène turn right and follow a scenic road upwards past the Cirque de St Amand. A backward look places Mont Ventoux's western end straight in front of you. Continue through Suzette, Lafare and the wine-village of Beaumes-de-Venise. A beautiful run at any time, it is specially so in early summer when the evening sun slants behind the Dentelles and sets the scented yellow masses of Spanish broom ablaze.

From Beaumes-de-Venice, the D81 and then the D7 turn into the road which runs on the west side of the Dentelles. On the right, a grass track leads to the rural chapel of Notre Dame d'Aubune whose tall, square belfry is ornamented with three fluted pilasters and carved decorations on each face, an unusual, much admired design.

Folk-legend has it that Charles Martel, having defeated the Saracens ouside Poitiers in 732, fought them again during their retreat in the vicinity of the Dentelles. The Saracens' Tower, said to be an eighth-century signal tower in ruins, is up the valley from the hamlet of Montmirail above the spring which once provided curative waters for a long-forgotten spa. The Saracens' Cemetery stands on a little plateau just above Notre Dame d'Aubune. There may be no historical reality in these names. It is just as likely that 'Saracen' refers to gypsies for, since the fifteenth century, the Provençaux, seeing a physical resemblance, have called gypsies 'Sarrasins', Saracens.

On the D23 is Gigondas, second only to Châteauneuf-du-Pape as a red wine of quality. The road continues past another delightful rural chapel of St Côme and St Damien whose external apse-roofs are covered with fish-tail tiles and the main roof is weighted with massive blocks to hold off the *mistral*. Higher still is Hôtel Les Florets, a centre for horse-riding, walking and rock-climbing.

After Sablet on its hillock, it is worth making a small detour uphill to Séguret, snuggling under a sheer wall of rock, for a stroll about its alleys, washhouse, old gateways and views over orchards and vines to the plain. A track leads back to Vaison.

The excursions from Vaison are far from exhausted. Many other villages are dotted about, each with its distinctive character, with its thick-walled houses, shady little squares and arches, and moss-covered fountain. Of all the sounds on a hot summer's day the most refreshing to the spirit (as well as hands and face) is the village fountain, that paradox of prodigally flowing water in a parched country. Mollans-sur-Ouvèze,

Part of Roman aqueduct, Pont du Gard

Triumphal Arch, Orange, a Roman masterpiece

Entrechaux, Roaix, Rasteau, Buisson are but some of the places which provide something fresh for camera and memory.

Next comes Orange and its Roman monuments. A Celtic capital, *Arausio*, it was colonised by veterans of the Roman Second Legion. They built the theatre, triumphal arch, temples, baths and other public buildings the colonists regarded as essential in their major cities.

For a general prospect of the town, the Rhône and the mountains, go to the top of Colline St Eutrope by the Montée des Princes d'Orange-Nassau.

At its foot is the Roman theatre whose circular tiers of seats were set into the hillside. The huge facade of red sandstone, 36m high and 103m long was said by Louis XIV to be 'the finest wall in my kingdom'. In its heyday, this magnificent stage backdrop in three tiers was decorated with seventy-six columns,

friezes, niches and statues. A great awning was held by poles; their supports are still visible. The statues have vanished save the one of Augustus, 3½m tall, discovered in fragments and pieced together, complete with his baton. It is placed high in the central niche, a Gaul grovelling for mercy at the Emperor's feet. The Romans were a little tactless in reminding the populace as to who their overlords were.

Vandals, time and wind may have eroded the wall, but the acoustics are still excellent. All the intricate ornamentation of the original wall and the sophisticated scene-shifting machinery are explained by the guide. An international music festival is held in the theatre during the last two weeks of July.

Close to the theatre are the excavations of a large Roman gymnasium, 400m long by 80m wide (the only one known in Gaul), with baths, athletics track and temples.

In the Municipal Museum opposite the theatre are items which have been removed during excavations. Perhaps the most interesting one is a cadastral plan engraved in AD 77. On a huge marble slab are recorded the configuration of the region, the boundaries of the properties of the Roman veterans and the Gaulish inhabitants (who had the poorest land). Names of owners, bondsmen, tax rates (six per cent surcharge on arrears!), show how efficient Roman bureaucracy was.

From the museum to the triumphal arch on foot is ³/₄ km. The large and considerably rebuilt twelfth-century ex-cathedral of Notre Dame is hardly out of the way.

The triumphal arch stands in the middle of a roundabout in the middle of the busy N7, at the northeast end of Orange. If it is a rather inconvenient site for today's visitor it is because the N7 is the modern version of the *Via Agrippa* to Lyon. Military and naval (the latter is unusual for the Romans) motifs are carved in rich profusion over the whole edifice to make it one of the masterpieces of the Roman Empire. Naked and hairy Gauls again give powerful advertisement to Roman mastery.

With two fine Roman monuments in mind, it is sensible to visit another splendid Roman construction in the vicinity, the Pont du Gard.

The D976 leaves Orange and almost immediately goes above the *Autoroute du Soleil* and runs more or less parallel to the other autoroute, *La Languedocienne*, which branches off at Orange. Keep right at Roquemaure and on through Remoulins to the Pont du Gard, 38km from Orange.

Whatever bias one may have about the imperious, sometimes stern and brutal rule imposed by the Romans, the sight of this great work goes far towards accepting Rome as a civilising influence.

Six lower arches span the wooded banks of the river Gardon. Above them are eleven wider, lighter arches by the side of which runs the roadway. Uppermot are thirty-five small arches, 275m long which carried the water-duct 2,000 years ago from the source of the Eure near Uzès to the Roman town of *Nemausus,* Nîmes, 50km away. 400 litres a day for every inhabitant of *Nemausus* was channelled over the Pont du Gard, more than is considered necessary today. For 400 years the conduit was regularly maintained before it fell into neglect and lime deposits choked the channel. In the nineteenth century, Napoleon III had the aqueduct restored.

Nearby is a large car park. The best views are from waymarked winding paths upstream. The conduit can be crossed on foot by those with a head for heights.

The Pont du Gard is a feast for the eyes: its setting, its bold dimensions, the warm colour of the rough, dressed drystone blocks. Its vitality and beauty derives from the fact that the arches are deliberately, though only slightly, irregular in span.

Back at Orange, an essential excursion for naturalists is to the village of Sérignan-du-Comtat. Go 3km along the N7 past the Roman arch; turn right on to the D976 and cross the vine-filled plain. On the outskirt of Sérignan is a high wall on the right behind which the entomologist Jean-Henri Fabre (1823-1915) lived and worked between 1879 and his death. 'The insects' Homer' is universally remembered by the translations of his important observations in the *Souvenirs*

Palace of the Popes, Avignon, from across the Rhône

entomologiques which give a lucid insight into the complex lives of the insects of Vaucluse, in a style both intimate and elegant. Fellow-scientists tended to dismiss him because of his refusal to accept Darwin's theory of evolution by natural selection; new views about the theory may rehabilitate Fabre and show that he was not the arch-reactionary he was held to be. The house and garden are a museum run by the Natural History Museum in Paris; his laboratory, collections, primitive equipment for research, and his child's writing desk are all on view. Fabre is buried in the cemetery outside Sérignan. His statue stands in the square.

The distance from Roman Orange to medieval Avignon is less than 30km. Take the D68 which in 10km reaches a village whose name is familiar to every wine-lover — Châteauneuf-du-Pape. Rows of green vines rise out of a sea of

PLACES TO VISIT FROM ORANGE

Pont du Gard: the Roman aqueduct.

Sérignan-du-Comtat: museum of J.H. Fabre, entomologist; fortified church.

Camaret: medieval gateway.

Mornas: ruined castle.

Bollène: Municipal Museum for drawings by Picasso and Chagall.

Barry: abandoned troglodytic village; view of nuclear installations and hydro-electric works, Donzère canal, Rhône, Ardèche hills.

Châteauneuf-du-Pape: vineyards; fourteenth-century castle.

large pebbles once rolled by the Rhône. They are a furnace which reflects the sun's heat on to the ripening grapes that produce a supple, warm, optimistic red wine in the making of which up to thirteen varieties of grape may be used.

Above the village are the imposing ruins of a fourteenth-century castle built by Pope John XXII as his summer residence. Plundered down the years, the last assault was by German troups which blew up most of the huge keep in 1944.

Avignon is a large town of 93,000 inhabitants; the great majority of them live outside the intact medieval ramparts. If outer Avignon is bustling and banal, the old town's narrow streets enclose the sense of history. The chief draw is the fortress-like fourteenth-century Palace of the Popes.

The Grand Courtyard of the Papal Palace is also the venue of the International Drama Festival during the last three weeks of July. Its great prestige draws enthusiasts from all over the world to see productions which some consider too *avant-garde* and élitist. However that may be, the Festival adds to Avignon's proverbial vitality — hence the old song about dancing on (though actually under) the bridge of Avignon.

A stroll through almost any part of old Avignon within the ramparts reveals the architectural styles of 200 and 300 years ago in the façades of mansions (*hôtels*) of wealthy merchants and the nobility. Two of the most picturesque streets are Rue Banasterie (Weavers' Row), and Rue des Teinturiers (Dyers' Row) where the river Sorgue flows gently past inert ancient mill wheels. Numerous churches and chapels of different periods are also scattered about the old town.

If there is a temptation to sentimentalise Avignon's past while gazing at its ancient remains, the

PLACES TO VISIT IN AVIGNON

Palace of the Popes, Place du Palais. Guided tours: Old Palace, Grand Courtyard, Consistory and Chapel, Banqueting Hall (Gobelin tapestries), St Martial Chapel (frescoes), Robing Room (Gobelin tapestries), Papal Bedchamber (frescoes of birds and animals), Room of the Deer (frescoes of hunting and fishing scenes), Clementine Chapel (statues and paintings). New Palace, Grand Audience Hall, Gallery of the Conclave.

Cathedral of Notre Dame-des-Doms, Place du Palais.

Rocher des Doms, rose gardens, lake, fine views across the Rhône.

Petit Palace Museum of medieval painting and sculpture, Place du Palais; thirteenth-century paintings of Avignon and Italian Schools.

Bridge of St Bénézet. Twelfth century, originally with twenty-two arches connecting Avignon with Villeneuve. Now only four remain plus Romanesque chapel of St Nicolas.

Calvet Museum, Rue Joseph Vernet. Mixed collections, Avignon School of painters; moderns; wrought-iron work; Hellenic sculptures, vases.

Lapidary Museum, 27 Rue de la République. Important local pre-Roman and Roman statuary, especially Gaulish *Tarasque of Noves* and *Venus of Pourrières*.

Pont St Bénézet, Avignon, four remaining arches over the Rhône

fulminations of one who served at the papal court — Petrarch — will restore the balance. He left to posterity his view that Avignon was a living hell, a sink of vice with neither faith, nor charity nor religion; the city was odious, pestilential when there was no *mistral*, insufferable when it blew.

Across the Rhône is Villeneuve-lès-Avignon (*lès* or *les* meaning 'near'), once connected by Pont St Bénézet to Avignon. Belonging to the Kingdom of France it was fortified by the French kings with the St André Fort and Tower of Philippe le Bel (the Fair) to keep frontier watch on Avignon which was part of the Holy Roman Empire. When the Popes came from Rome to Avignon,

PLACES TO VISIT IN VILLENEUVE-LES-AVIGNON

Tower of Philippe le Bel.

Fort of St André and abbey.

Municipal Museum, whose chief glory is the *Coronation of the Virgin* (1453) painted by Enguerrand Charanton (the surname is variously spelled).

Charterhouse of Val de Bénédiction, see particularly frescoes by Matteo Giovanetti, fourteenth century painter at the Papal Palace.

Church of Notre Dame, with outstanding fourteenth century *Virgin and Child* carved from an elephant's tusk.

the cardinals chose the salubrious rising ground of Villeneuve to build their summer palaces, most of which were destroyed at the time of the Revolution.

Villeneuve is a quieter place to stay than Avignon. To stand at the top of Philippe le Bel's tower as the sun begins to set throws Avignon and the Papal Palaces into a warm relief and illuminates the distant hump of Mont Ventoux.

2 Upper Provence and the Durance Valley

From the direction of Grenoble two routes make for the heart of Provence. One is the N75 which goes over the Col de la Croix Haute (1,176m) in the Devoluy range to Serres. The other, more easterly road, is the N85 which traverses the Col Bayard (1,246m) in the Champsaur range, and leads to Gap. They converge just north of Sisteron.

Sisteron is a theatrical gateway into Provence. The harsh Dauphiné mountains are to the north, and to the south the valley opens on to richer, warmer land. Buckled, striated mountains have been narrowly breached at Sisteron by the Durance which has brought down tons of debris from one-time glaciers which never moved further south than Sisteron.

Clearly destined for strategic importance throughout history, Sisteron last suffered from Allied air attacks in 1944 when some of the medieval quarters were destroyed. They have been reconstructed.

Near the Place de la République (where cars can be parked) are the town hall, church, and the four remaining fifteenth-century towers whose ramparts have all but disappeared. Old Sisteron Museum is also close by; its archaeological items were retrieved during reconstruction work.

The full name of the one-time cathedral is Notre Dame-des-Pommiers (nothing to do with apples, but a corruption of *pomerium,* an area which must be left free). Its architecture reflects Sisteron's geographical position; Lombard and Alpine influences show in the octagonal tower and its external gallery. The perfect alignment of the masonry is characterically Provençal.

A warren of narrow streets, stepped and vaulted (*andrônes*), linking tiny squares, make up the old quarters. Where the main street enters a tunnel is a bust of Paul Arène (1843-96), a Sisteron writer of lightness and charm who, under a pseudonymn, wrote the famous *Lettres de mon moulin* with Alphonse Daudet in 1866.

The citadel of massive ancient fortifications, started in the eleventh century and added to later, stands

---

EXCURSIONS FROM SISTERON

East of the Durance

Valley of Sasse — La Motte — Turriers — Col des Sagnes (1,182m) — Bayons — Clamensane — Nibles.

Col de la Sacristie — Défilé de Pierre Ecrite (large fifth-century Roman inscription carved on roadside rock, dedicated to Dardanus, Prefect of the Gauls, who constructed this road) — St Geniez — Col de Fontbielle (1,304m) — Mélan Forest — Thoard — Mallemoisson — Volonne.

West of the Durance

Valley of Jabron — Noyers-sur-Jabron — Séderon — Gorges de la Méouge — Ribiers.

Both east and west of Sisteron is good walking country.

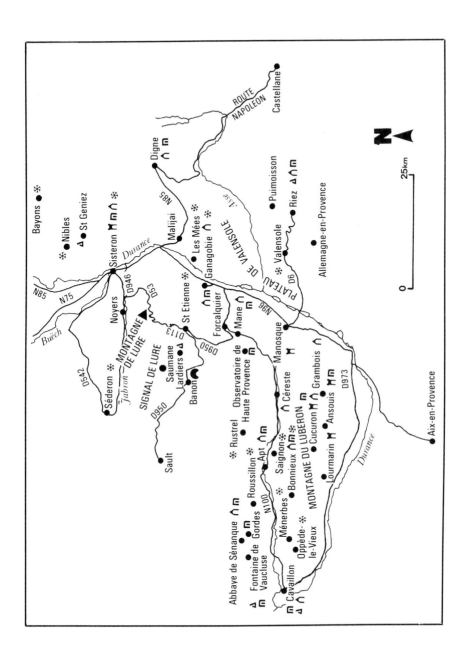

*Sisteron, the rock breached by the river Durance where it enters Provence from
Dauphiné*

supreme above the town. A curtain wall on a narrow ridge and supported by high arches leads to the citadel which is reached by a steep walk, the reward for which is a panorama whose features are identified on a viewing table. Both citadel and rock are floodlit on summer evenings, when broadcasts in French explain Sisteron's history. In the guardroom at the entrance is a museum of local wartime resistance.

Numerous excursions to both east and

west of the Durance can be undertaken. The eastern ones are more alpine in character for they penetrate valleys whose peaks are over 2,000m, while the more open valleys to the west are Mediterranean in aspect.

In a region of small towns, Digne, west of Sisteron, with 16,500 inhabitants, is a popular stopping place well supplied with hotels. It is also a spa for the treatment of rheumatism.

Its mountainous setting of steep and sombre crags imparts a sense of desolation and makes Digne more alpine than Provençal.

Boulevard Gassendi in Ville-Haute is the main artery of activity and interest. On each side of it are car parks. At one end is the Grande Fontaine, its Doric structure buried under tufa and moss. At the centre of the Boulevard is Place Charles de Gaulle and a statue of Pierre Gassendi (1592-1655), philosopher and polymath, born at nearby Champtercier.

The old part lies to one side of Boulevard Gassendi. The Municipal Museum, housed in a one-time hospice, provides a visual survey of Digne's prehistory and the Gallo-Roman period. Paintings by local artists are augmented by better-known painters such as Natoire and Ziem. A natural history collection includes specimens of unusual local lepidoptera.

Notre Dame-du-Bourg, once a cathedral, stands at the northern outskirts, and Lombard and Alpine influences are apparent, as at Sisteron. This majestic building has a particularly fine rose window, but the church is used now only for funerals; the caretaker at the cemetery has to be found in order to get in.

Digne is the capital of a vast area where lavender is grown. In July an international lavender-essence fair takes place. Four kinds of lavender grow in Provence. True (or common) lavender, from which the finest essence is distilled; aspic, flowering in late August, is not cultivated but hybridises with true lavender to give *lavandin* which yields great quantities of inferior essence. Lastly, French lavender, found mainly on silica soils like the Maures mountains, has deep purple flowers but is of no commercial value.

Places other than Sisteron or Digne suggest themselves as centres for short stays. Manosque and Forcalquier have a town atmosphere; Valensole and St Etienne are villages where the countryside comes to the doorstep. Gréoux-les-Bains, although primarily a spa where arthritis and lesions are treated, has pleasant hotels.

As a peaceful excursion centre with modest but agreeable hotel facilities St Etienne (St Etienne-les-Orgues on some maps) has my preference. From Sisteron an attractive secondary road, D951, passing the villages of Mallefougasse and Cruis, goes to St Etienne at the foot of the southern slope of Montagne de Lure.

Lure is the natural extension of Mont Ventoux, separated from it by the depression at Sault. It, too, is a limestone mass riddled with underground caves (*dolines*) into which streams vanish abruptly.

Walkers will climb the Lure on foot and find many tracks along its crest and flanks. A motor road also goes to the top and over the north side. The D113 leaves St Etienne's open valley, climbs through oaks and conifers. At the roadside Oratories of St Joseph, a path descends to the right to the Lure Hermitage, founded in 500 by St Donat, now a small Romanesque chapel surrounded by old lime trees.

The road goes no higher than 1,700m. A steep climb reaches the Signal de Lure

(1,827m) where the panorama is unbroken. Some dwarf juniper, beech and gorse are scattered near the barren summit. Saxifrages, fritillaries and Mont Cenis violets appear as soon as the snows melt. Later come orchids. Butterflies are quite plentiful; 70 per cent of them are alpine or central European and Asiatic.

A brusque, zigzag descent goes into the Jabron valley, though this section of road is closed between mid-November and the end of May.

Of motoring excursions out of St Etienne, two attractive roads go to Forcalquier, while a longer westward journey aims for Banon, 2km from which is one of the deepest caves in France. The Gouffre du Caladaïre, some 480m deep, is reached on foot, and to the left is the romantically abandoned village of Montsalier-le-Vieux.

Or, by turning right 9km out of St Etienne in the Banon direction, the D12 leads to tiny Lardiers. On a nearby hilltop are the remains of an important Gallo-Roman shrine, the *oppidum* of Chastelard-de-Lardiers. A double wall enclosed some 20 acres which surrounded a sanctuary. Vast deposits of gold, silver and bronze rings and 50,000 tiny clay lamps — all votive offerings to Mercury, patron of travellers — have been excavated.

The road from Lardiers continues north to Saumane, and then swings back to Banon. Simiane-la-Rotonde, 10km southwest, has a curious, lantern-like, twelfth-century hexagonal tower — a keep and chapel combined — built into the remains of a castle, and furnished with a cone-like roof. Inside, the edifice is irregularly twelve-sided by means of twelve blind arcades. Below is a crypt; above, an ornamented chamber. Stairs built in the thick walls give access to

Simiane-la-Rotonde, 12th century hexagonal tower crowning the village

Manosque, fourteenth-century fortified gateway of Porte Saunerie

upper terraces of this strange building.

Some say the lords of Simiane built the *rotonde* in imitation of the castles erected by Crusaders in the Holy Land. Others think it is a likeness to the circular kitchens of medieval abbeys. Enquire for the key in the village.

A stay at Forcalquier (*Furnus calcarius* in the Middle Ages when local limekilns kept the men in work) usually begins with a visit to the impressive but darkly brooding church of Notre Dame, begun in 1196. In front is a fifteenth-century fountain surmounted by an octagonal pinnacle with a plaque commemorating the marriage in 1235 of Eleanore of Provence to Henry III of England.

Manosque, belfry of St Sauveur, typical 18th century wrought-ironwork

On market days the square in front of Notre Dame is thronged with stalls. Nearby are the local archaeological museum and the restored Franciscan monastery, founded in 1236. A walk through the old quarters where there was once a Jewish community and a synagogue leads to the citadel from whose terraces are fine views.

Forcalquier's cemetery, about 1km north of the town, is sufficiently unusual for a French cemetery that it is a tourist attraction in its own right. Terraces are lined by tall and ancient yews neatly clipped and shaped into arched niches and topiaries. It contains small, cylindrical, drystone buildings with pointed roofs called *cabanons*.

Villages of charm lie in all directions, such as St Maime, Dauphin (a good example of a perched village), Limans, Sigonces.

The Priory of Ganagobie is reached by a winding road from the N96 on the right bank of the Durance. From the tree-filled plateau is a balcony view of the valley. The Benedictine Monastery was founded in 980, rebuilt in the twelfth century, to be partially destroyed in 1792. A Christ in Majesty decorates the lintel of the striking main doorway. A triple arch, decorated with oriental-looking festoonery, surrounds the door.

A guide shows the profane twelfth-century mosaics, and a Virgin in the nave painted by Adolphe Monticelli (1824-86) who spent his orphaned childhood at Ganagobie. Although this is not one of his better paintings, it is a reminder that this highly original artist whose jewel-like brushwork fired Van Gogh with admiration, was responsible for the Dutchman coming to Provence for two momentous years.

Manosque, 23km south of Forcalquier, and set above the sluggish coils of the Durance, has a population of 19,500, and offers a range of hotels within and round about the town. It has grown rapidly as the marketing centre for early vegetables, fruit and truffles, and as the place of residence for workers at the Cadarache nuclear power station downstream where the Verdon joins the Durance.

Two fourteenth-century fortified gateways, Porte Saunerie and Porte Soubeyran, mark the bounds of the old town. A handsomely wrought iron

belfry surmounts the square tower of St Sauveur church. Such eighteenth-century campaniles are common in Provence and are poetically spoken of as 'God's sheep bells'.

Northeastwards, Manosque rises to the Mont d'Or, the place where the novelit Jean Giono (1895-1970) lived for most of his life. Many of his novels use his native landscape as elemental forces; readers of these books will conjure vivid images from the names that recur in them: Vachères, Banon, Le Revest-du-Bion, Ste Tulle and Manosque itself. Giono is buried in Manosque's cemetery.

Cross the Durance canal and river by the D907 and take the D6 which rises through wooded country to the open plateau of undulating hills covered by bristling rows of lavender and almond trees round Valensole. Distant peaks jut coyly beyond the rim of the plateau, and the Luberon range, across the Durance, is a luminous blue in this limpid light.

When the Burgundians invaded this part of Provence, Riez was *Reia Apollinaris,* an important administrative centre in the Roman Empire. Coming from Valensole, on the right are four columns of grey granite with Corinthian capitals and an architrave of white marble, the remains of a first-century Roman temple, presumably dedicated to Apollo. The nearest quarry of grey granite was at Pennafort near Callas in Var, 117km away.

Another uncommon relic is the baptistry at the edge of Riez on the road to Allemagne-en-Provence (from *Alemona,* a fertility goddess). Experts disagree about when it was erected; some say in the fourth century, others, the seventh century. Outside it is square with a later dome; it is octagonal within with four apsidal chapels let into the thickness of the walls. A ruined

Rochers des Mées, flock on traditional route to high summer pastures

baptismal font is surrounded by eight
Corinthian columns of grey granite (as
at the temple), again, surmounted by
marble capitals. A collection of
sarcophagi, a taurobolic altar, slabs with
inscriptions, carved masks and
fragments of pillars can be seen through
the iron grille.

There are some charming places in
Riez, and a sundial of 1806 in Place St
Antoine bears a reflective message, 'The
most serene moment is marked by a
shadow'.

North of Riez lies an empty corner of
Provence where the valley of the Asse
cuts the Plateau de Valensole in two.
One or two farm roads meander across
this severer part of the plateau. To
savour this isolation take the D953 past
Puimoisson, then the D8 northwards
from Bras d'Asse through the Ravin des
Caraires to reach the river Bléone
opposite Malijai on the *Route Napoléon.*
Continue on the D6 for 5km until a long
aligment of conglomerate rocks appear.
They are the Rochers des Mées (from the
Latin *metae,* milestones), or more
popularly, the Pénitents Blancs, for the

line of high rocks looks like a procession of cowled figures detached from the hillformation behind them by erosion.

West of Manosque is the Montagne du Luberon, like other Provençal ranges pointing east-west and gently concave in the middle. It is a Regional Park aimed at conserving its natural assets.

A much more intimate mountain than either Ventoux or Lure, Luberon is 65km long, divided into Grand Luberon east of the Combe de Lourmarin with

---

PLACES TO VISIT IN THE LUBERON MOUNTAINS

Ansouis: seventeenth-century château, exhibits of armoury, furniture, tapestries. Museum of Provençal furniture and underwater life.

La Bastide-des-Jourdans: some fortified gateways; ruins of ancient monastery; remains of chapel of Knights Templars.

Bonnieux: nineteenth-century church with fifteenth century paintings of German School; twelfth century church, cedar trees, views; old streets, fountains.

Castellet: hillside hamlet.

Cucuron: church; belfry; fifteenth century château; old streets; Luberon museum.

Grambois: solid old buildings at different levels; restored Romanesque church, paintings in chapel.

Lacoste: eighteenth-century château of Marquis de Sade being restored.

Lauris: views of Durance from ramparts.

Lourmarin: fifteenth-century Renaissance château; cemetery, graves of novelist Albert Camus

(1913-60) and Henri Bosco (1888-1976) (like Jean Giono wove spirit of Provençal countryside into novels and poems).

Maubec: remains of medieval castle.

Ménerbes: old village; church; citadel; views.

Oppède-le-Vieux: picturesque village being restored; fine views.

Saignon: at foot of isolated rock; church.

St Symphorien Priory: solitary, elegant square Romanesque belfry on limestone rocks near Bonnieux.

La Tour d'Aigues: monumental doorway of ruined château built 1570, abandoned 1792.

Scenic roads
Manosque — La Bastide-des-Jourdans — Vitrolles — crest of Grand Luberon — Mourre Nègre — Cucuron.

Céreste — la Bégude — Castellet — Auribeau — Saignon — Apt.

Cadenet — Lourmarin — Buoux — Apt.

Bonnieux — Massif des Cèdres — Cavaillon.

Bonnieux at the col, and Petit Luberon to the west. Once a walker's preserve, a road along the crest of Grand Luberon has more recently opened out the luminous vistas to the motorist.

There is an almost secret atmosphere. Dozens of varied villages repay a visit; no two are alike in character and architecture, though many have shared the suffering of sixteenth-century massacres. Members of the Vaudois sect, followers of the twelfth-century fundamentalist Petrus Valdo, seeking to escape persecution in Piedmont, settled in the Luberon in the fourteenth century. The Popes at Avignon declared the Vaudois to be heretics and the repression of their 10,000 homes took place in 1545 with fanatical inhumanity. Some of the villages were never allowed to be rebuilt, their names extirpated from maps and records. Old Mérindol, the religious centre of the Vaudois, is still just a heap of stones.

Cavaillon, on the right bank of the Durance, is in the flatlands at the foot of the Petit Luberon. It is a thriving commercial centre for the early season fruit and vegetable market, and its name is associated with fragrant pink melons. At least five places are worth making for in Cavaillon.

The thirteenth-century former cathedral of St Véran is a good example of the Provençal style. A pentagonal external apse is dominated by an octagonal tower. All the side chapels contain paintings and carvings in wood and stone.

Walk along the Grand' Rue from the church to enter the Municipal Museum with a display of prehistoric finds, a reconstruction of Cavaillon's Roman arch, and a room showing 500 Greek, Gaulish and Roman coins found on Colline St Jacques above the town.

At Rue Chabran is a beautifully preserved eighteenth-century synagogue. What were known as the four Holy Communities of Avignon, Carpentras, l'Isle-sur-la-Sorgue and Cavaillon, ensured the protection of Jews from early in the fourteenth century until the French Revolution, so that the Comtat Venaissin came to be known as 'the Jewish paradise' under the direct authority of the Popes, and administered by elected chiefs called *baylons*. Below the synagogue, in the part reserved for making unleaven bread, is a small Judeo-Comtadin museum. The Roman arch of the first century in Place du Clos, was moved stone by stone in 1880 from the wall of St Véran church in which it had been embedded. Unlike arches commemorating victories, this one is richly decorated but conspicuously lacking military motifs.

From Place du Clos, a 15-minute walk up a stepped path arrives at the top of the abrupt rock of Colline St Jacques. Neolithic and Ligurian tribes inhabited the site on which the seventeenth century chapel of St Jacques now stands. Then it became a powerful Celtic *oppidum*. Later, the Greeks of *Massalia* (Marseille) set up a trading post for their goods to be carried up the Durance by boatmen who were the forerunners of the powerful guilds formed under Roman rule. In about 42BC the Romans founded *Cabellio* in the plain below.

The distance between Forcalquier and Cavaillon is 73km, almost all on N100, and a number of tempting diversions to the north of the road (the Luberon is to the south) present themselves on the way.

Near Mane, the first village, is the empty twelfth-century Notre Dame-de-Salagon priory with its simple portal and carved capitals depicting the baptism of Christ, standing in a field. Further along the road is the elegant eighteenth-

Sénanque Abbey which contains a Saharan exhibition

century Château de Sauvan.

A turning leads to the Haute Provence Observatory which can be visited on certain days in summer. Another road leads to perched Reillanne.

To the west is Céreste, enclosed in its walls, while a valley road goes to Carluc Priory, an early Christian necropolis cut out of its rock.

Apt is next, the Celto-Ligurian town of *Hath* before Julius Caesar made it *Apta Julia,* now known for its crystallised fruits.

Two archaic crypts, one above the other, are the curiosity in the church of Ste Anne. The upper was hollowed out in the eleventh century; an altar of earlier date rests on a Gallo-Roman monumental pillar or *cippus.* Six diminutive thirteenth-century ossuarial sarcophagi fit neatly into niches.

In the lower crypt, the relics of Ste Anne, mother of the Virgin Mary, brought from Palestine, were supposed to have come to light here in 776, the year Charlemagne came to consecrate, so it is said, the earlier church on this site.

Archaeologists have unearthed fourth-century Christian sarcophagi in the vicinity, so where St Anne stands was one of the earliest organised Christian communities in the whole of Gaul. Also, this may have been the first church in the Occident to venerate the Virgin's mother. The original church was erected in the fifth century using the foundations of a Roman temple. Apt became a place of pilgrimage. Anne of Austria came here in 1623, prayed to be made fertile (it took fifteen years for the wish to be realised), and bequeathed valuable reliquaries which are in the treasury and Ste Anne's chapel.

Close to the church, in Rue de l'Amphithéâtre, is the Archaeological Museum of local Roman items, including a fragment of the arena, and faïence ware.

The best preserved Roman bridge in France, Pont Julien, is reached by going 8km west from Apt along the N100; then turn left on to the Bonnieux road which almost at once crosses the hump-back of the bridge over the river Coulon. It was built in the first century AD to carry the *Via Domitia* across what must then have been a turbulent stream, for the pillars of the three powerful arches have openings which allowed floodwater to flow more freely and relieved stress on the structure.

Take the Pont Julien road (D108) north to Roussillon, surrounded by now-abandoned quarry pits of various ochre colours, the most startling one being an intense red-brown. All these shades appear on the façades of the houses.

More quarries of grey, green and pink marl occur near Gargas, east of Roussillon. These are still worked.

Even more spectacular are the iron-oxide quarries near Rustrel, about 19km east via St Saturnin-d'Apt on the edge of the Plateau de Vaucluse. Rustrel Colorado can be visited on foot after leaving the car near the Dôa stream. Columns of red ochre, capped with clay like giant mushrooms, are bizarre features in the landscape.

Back at Roussillon, a village clambering up a hillside, 10km away to the west, can be seen. This is Gordes.

PLACES TO VISIT NEAR GORDES

Village Noir: deserted bories (beehive-shaped drystone huts). Take D15 towards Cavaillon; path on right to car park. Distance 1½km.
 Bories village and museum of traditional rural life: go beyond junction of D15 and D2, then 2km of rough track. Distance 3km.

Stained Glass Museum: modern building next to sixteenth-century Bouillons olive mill. Follow D2, left at Belvedere. Distance 5km. History of stained glass and exhibition, especially of work by Frédérique Duran.

Sénanque Abbey: D177 north for 4km, left for 1km in valley of Sénanque. Cistercian abbey, one of three famous 'sisters of Provence' with Silvacane and Le Thoronet. See abbey buildings and permanent exhibition of all aspects of Sahara desert.

Resurgent river Sorgue at Fontaine de Vaucluse

Dying in the 1920s, revived under the impulsion of the artist, André Lhote, damaged by war in 1944, Gordes now flourishes and attracts many visitors.

Loftily perched is its Renaissance château, like others in Provence a mixture of medieval and Renaissance, with finely proportioned rooms, decorations, stairway and exuberant chimney-piece. In it is the striking Vasarely Museum. The versatile, Hungarian-born artist Vasarely, who restored the château, has installed his didactic museum with some 1,000 of his own works. Abstract, undulating designs of pure colour express his notion of continuous movement. Also on show are some of his earlier figurative works.

To reach the Fontaine de Vaucluse from Gordes, take the D15, the Cavaillon road, turning right after 6km to Cabrières-d'Avignon, then the D100 and D100A to the village of Fontaine de Vaucluse.

The 'fountain' is the resurgent river Sorgue which appears as a lake at the cavernous foot of a huge semi-circular crag where *son et lumière* shows are given on summer evenings. Aloft is the ruined castle of the bishops of Cavaillon. What looks like a placid lake and stream turns into a foaming torrent after heavy rains in winter and spring have seeped into the fissured limestone rocks of Mont Ventoux, Lure and Luberon. The underground streams come to the surface through this powerful siphon.

The remains of the Roman aqueduct which carried the waters of the Sorgues to Arles are visible by the roadside of the D24 near the village of Galas.

In Fontaine de Vaucluse itself is the Norbert Casteret Speleological Museum; it contains material relating to Casteret's 30 years of exploration, sometimes dangerous, to solve the mystery of the subterranean passages beneath the emerald green waters of the resurgent Sorgue.

The column in the square honours the poet Petrarch who retired to this spot from Avignon between 1327 and 1353 to write many of the poems which speak of his unrequited love for Laura of Avignon, and his attachment to the solitude (as it then was) of Fontaine de Vaucluse (his *Vallis Clausa,* the Closed Valley). A small Petrarch museum stands on what is thought to be the site of his house. Over the centuries men of letters have come here in pilgrimage in respect for a major innovative poet, and his romantic attachment to Laura. He has been called the first modern man who took the first step away from medievalism's fearful submission to divine authority towards the individualistic Renaissance assertion of man as the measurer of values.

Gorges du Verdon

Barrage du Verdon

Port Cros, Iles d'Hyères

3 Arles and the Camargue

North of Arles the Rhône bifurcates to make a triangular delta bounded on the east by the Grand Rhône, and the Petit Rhône on the west. Some 40km separate the two estuaries which empty into the Golfe du Lion. In this triangle is the Camargue.

Round its periphery are towns with ancient monuments, and subtle landscapes. The region clings to traditions evolved during a long period of isolation.

Arles, 38km south of Avignon, is a popular centre, full of reminders of its illustrious past. It was the first Roman foundation in Gaul. 'The granary of Rome' it was known as, and later, 'the little Rome of the Gauls'. Now it is a museum city of its Roman and medieval heritage. Savour its atmosphere on foot; a car is no help in the narrow streets.

Start with the tree-lined Boulevard des Lices, thoroughly modern, it is true, with thronged cafés and restaurants. Make for Place de la République where stands a Roman obelisk of Egyptian stone, moved here from the chariot race-course in the suburb of Trinquetaille.

On one side of the *place* is the seventeenth-century Hôtel de Ville; on another is the west façade of St Trophime church. The west porch is a delight of Romanesque art. Elaborate carvings in great rhythmical patterns borrowed motifs from Syrian, Persian, Nordic and antique Roman sources.

Rooftops of old Arles

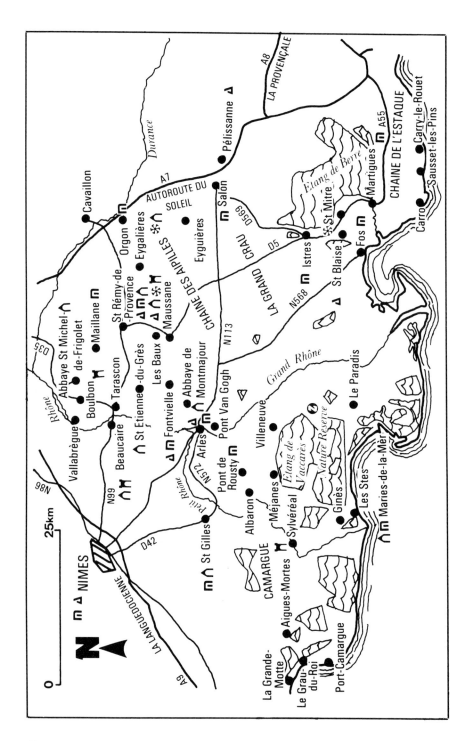

Detail of early sarcophagus in Museum of Christian Art, Arles

Illiterate pilgrims on their way to St James of Compostela in Spain received the carved messages of election and damnation as effectively as a television advertisement today. The interior is equally fine and strong. An unusually narrow nave lends exaggerated height to the vaults. Paintings, Aubusson tapestries, carvings in wood and ivory and sarcophagi adorn the church.

To the right of St Trophime, in the one-time Archbishop's Palace, is the Tourist Information Office.

Just north of Place de la République is the small and shady Place du Forum in which stands a statue of the poet Frédéric Mistral; the wrought iron-work surrounding it is in the form of a *ficheiroun* or trident traditionally used by the cowboys or *gardians* of the Camargue. Embedded in the angle of the wall of the venerable Hôtel Nord-Pinus are two Corinthian columns which once formed part of a temple adjoining the Roman forum.

The Place du Forum is a reminder of Vincent van Gogh's brief stay in Arles

A single ticket admits to eight museums, all open 8.30am or 9am to 12 noon; 2-5.30pm or 7.30pm, according to season.

Amphitheatre (Arènes), Rond Point des Arènes. Twelfth in size of seventy known in Roman world. Held up to 15,000 spectators. Probably built in latter part of first century AD on site of wooden arena. Beast-cages below. Fortress in Middle Ages; two towers still stand. Bullfights on alternate Sundays, April-November; festival over Easter.

Roman theatre (Théâtre Antique), Rue du Cloître. Built in reign of Augustus with sumptuous decorations, statues, marble facings, seating 7,500. Pillaged in Middle Ages.

Museum of Christian Art (Musée d'Art Chrétien), Rue Balze. Best collection of sarcophagi outside Rome's. Many taken from Alyscamps. Below is Cryptoporticus, U-shaped tunnels built by Greeks to store grain.

Museum of Pagan Art (Musée d'Art Païen), Rue de la République. Local Greek and Roman art. Includes statue of Augustus and casts of Venus of Arles (original in Louvre) from Théâtre Antique.

Les Alyscamps, Allées des Sarcophages. Path lined with sarcophagi, residue of necropolis famed from Roman to medieval times. Ruined Romanesque church of St Honorat at end.

Musée Réattu, Rue du Grand Prieuré. Large collections of fine arts to present day: tapestries, furniture, ceramics, local and major artists, photographs, seventy drawings by Picasso. Behind museum promenade along bank of Rhône.

Trouille Roman Baths (Thermes de la Trouille, Palais Constantin), Rue D. Maïsto. Baths of Constantine the Great's imperial palace of fourth century. Water brought 25km from Eygalières by aqueduct.

St Trophime Cloisters (Cloître St Trophime), Place de la République (entrance through Tourist Office). Elegant, richly carved cloisters surrounding small garden. Twelfth- to fourteenth-century chapel with seventeenth-century tapestries.

---

between February 1888 and May 1889, when his painting reached full maturity. His *Café Terrace at Night* is now a furniture shop. *The Yellow House* in Place Lamartine, which he shared with Gauguin, was destroyed by bombs in 1944. The cemetery of the Alyscamps remains much as when he painted it. The famous drawbridge (erected by an earlier Dutchman) over the Marseille au Rhône Canal just south of Arles, sketched and painted by Vincent into immortality, was pulled down in 1926, but reconstructed later. Nor does one see the Arlesian costumes he painted, save on rather self-conscious folkloric days.

Most of the museums may be visited with one ticket, but one major museum,

One ticket admits to places below.
Guided tours all year.

Amphitheatre (Arènes), Boulevard Victor Hugo. Smaller than that at Arles but better preserved. Roman gladiatorial combats, chariot races. Spanish and Provençal bullfights Sundays, May-October.

Maison Carrée, Boulevard Victor Hugo. Temple in Hellenic style built just before beginning of our era; finest surviving Roman temple. Walled sanctum (*cella*) contains important Museum of Antiquities.

Fountain Gardens (Jardins de la Fontaine), Quai de la Fontaine. Ornamental eighteenth-century French garden, Nemausus springs, vestiges of Roman baths, ruined Temple of Diana.

Tour Magne, Mont Cavalier (behind Jardins de la Fontaine). Octagonal watch-tower of 1BC. Extensive views from platform on top.

Castellum, Rue de la Lampèze. Roman collecting basin for water from Pont du Gard, distribution point by ten canals to city of *Nemausus.* Only similar construction at Pompei.

Porte d'Arles, Place Gabriel Péri. 16BC Roman gateway in town walls.

See also:

Museum of Old Nîmes (Musée de Vieux-Nîmes), Place aux Herbes. Furniture, clothing, looms, history of bullfighting.

Museum of Archaeology (Musée d'Archéologie), Boulevard Amiral Courbet. Prehistory museum, natural history museum.

Fine Arts Museum (Musée des Beaux-Arts), Rue de la Cité-Foulc. Many schools and periods of painting.

Museon Arlaten, Rue de la République, lies outside the collective ticket scheme. Created in 1896 by the traditionalist poet Mistral as 'the true museum of the living life and people of Arles', and enlarged with the money he won as Nobel Prize Laureate for Literature in 1904, he packed the thirty rooms with anything (labelled in Provençal by his own hand) which recorded the culture of his beloved *pays d'Arles.* From herbs to costumes, poems to furniture, theatre programmes to life-size tableaux: here is yesteryear's Provence.

By visiting St Gilles and Nîmes in

Gard the Roman and medieval impressions gained in Arles are extended.

St Gilles, 16km west of Arles on the N572, was also a stopping-place for pilgrims on their way to St James of Compostela. Three rounded doors fill the width of the west front of the abbey-church; the effect is even more impressive than the one at St Trophime. The carvings surrounding them were done in the late twelfth and early thirteenth centuries and depict scenes from the life of Christ. St Gilles' tomb is in the crypt which is an early example

Nîmes, exterior of Roman arena

(eleventh century) of ogival vaulting.
A belfry contains a spiral staircase —
le Vis de St Gilles — whose fifty steps are
roofed with stone like a curving tunnel,
an early example of the stonemason's
craft. Items removed from the church

are displayed in the nearby museum.
North-west from St Gilles, the D42
passes the Garons airfield and enters
Nîmes.
St Rémy-de-Provence, with a
population of 8,000 is also a popular

Brun, in a handsome sixteenth-century mansion, has some souvenirs of the man who became physician to Charles IX, and was struck off for keeping his remedies secret. Turning to astrology, he wrote his highly obscurantist *Centuries,* quatrains of predictions which impressed Catherine de Medicis. He finished up rich and famous.

The museum also contains collections of local traditional art, and souvenirs of Frédéric Mistral who lived all his life in Maillane, 7km away, where the house he lived in from 1876 to his death in 1914 is now a substantial Museon Mistral.

A second museum, Musée Lapidaire, Rue du Parège, in Hôtel de Sade, once the home of relatives of the notorious sadistic marquis, should be looked at after a visit to the archaeological site of *Glanum,* as many items from there are shown in the museum.

Go first to see two Roman monuments whose grace will delight the eye even of those not interested in antiquities. Less than 2km south of St Rémy, on the right-hand side of the D5, they are unenclosed, surrounded by turf and trees. Their lightness and delicacy betray a Greek influence. One is the municipal arch of around 20BC the oldest and smallest to survive in southern France. It stood at the entrance to the town of *Glanum* on the other side of the road, and the *Via Domitia* highway passed under it. The reliefs commemorate Julius Caesar's victories over the Gauls and Greeks of *Massalia* in 49BC, but there is a more mellow feature, too: a Gaul being granted his freedom. Next to the arch is the beautifully preserved little mausoleum in memory of Julius Caesar's two adopted sons.

In *Glanum,* excavations have revealed the presence of Neolithic, Ligurian and Gaulish settlers before Phoenician

centre for its choice of hotels, its setting close to the Alpilles hills, and the fruit and market-gardens which surround it.

The most famous of all astrologers, Michel de Nostradamus (1503-66) was born here, and Musée Alpilles Pierre de traders named the place *Glanon,* and later Caesar Romanised it to *Glanum.* Houses with fine mosaics, a forum, baths, temples, nymphaeum, can be seen in this extensive open-air museum where much remains to be uncovered.

On the return to St Rémy, turn in to the Priory of St Paul de Mausole. Vincent van Gogh became a voluntary patient here in 1889-90 and continued in periods of lucidity to paint as expressively as before. Only his bust in the drive is a reminder of the event. Do not miss seeing the richly carved capitals of the twelfth-century cloisters.

The Chaîne des Alpilles, bare white limestone formations eroded into striking sculpted forms dominate the otherwise flat, well-irrigated landscape. They give an impression of height and grandeur, though they nowhere reach

500m. A round tour of 80km reveals the loveliest parts; walkers can cross the chain on the GR6 pathway: Eyguières, Aureille, Eygalières, the peak of La Caume, Les Baux, St Gabriel.

For most visitors, Les Baux is the main objective. Best approached by the D27 from St Rémy, this extraordinary village is hardly distinguishable from the spur of naked rock in which it is set. It may have been the inspiration for Dante's *Inferno.*

Prehistoric man has left traces of his safe *oppidum.* More is known of the Lords of Les Baux who, from the eleventh to the fifteenth centuries were powerful far beyond the confines of Provence, a history mostly of brigandage save for the thirteenth century, when Les Baux was famous for its 'Courts of Love' and the troubadours

On Plateau des Antiques outside St Rémy-de-Provence: Municipal Arch of 20BC and Mausoleum in memory of Julius Caesar's two adopted sons

Medieval village of Les Baux almost indistinguishable from rocks of Alpilles

who performed there.

In the seventeenth century it embraced Protestatism; Louis XIII and Richelieu had the castle and ramparts destroyed so that a once populous town began to crumble into decay.

Today, the rituals of the sixteenth-century Midnight Mass (*pastrage*) — symbolic of pastoral Provence — are kept movingly alive each Christmas Eve in the church of St Vincent, when it is packed.

Bauxite, discovered here in 1822 as a vital mineral from which aluminium is extracted, perpetuates the name of Les Baux, although the major bauxite quarries are elsewhere in central Provence.

16km west of St Rémy on the N99 is Tarascon. Its massive, fifteenth-century moated castle — an outstanding example of medieval fortification — is well preserved and rears above the

Rhône to defy the castle of Beaucaire on the opposite bank: independent Provence confronting the Kingdom of France. Elegant upper rooms served as appartments of royalty for banquets and entertainment by strolling troubadours.

Close by is the restored twelfth-century church of Ste Marthe, which is said to contain her remains. Legend has it that the saint, coming from the Camargue, vanquished the *tarasque*, a monster which terrified the town and devoured its children. She, by giving the sign of the Cross, pacified it and, placing her girdle round its neck, led it to the Rhône to vanish for ever. A festival, decreed by King René in 1496, has been kept alive on the last Sunday in June when a papier-mâché *tarasque* is paraded with much jollification — Christianity's triumph over Paganism.

North of Tarascon on the D35 is Boulbon on the slopes of the

73

Enter on foot by **Porte Mage.**

Town Hall. seventeenth century.

Eyguières Gate.

St Vincent Square. View over Val d'Enfer, luxury hotels, Queen Jeanne Pavilion, a small Renaissance building reached on foot from Eyguières Gate.

Hôtel des Porcelets (Archaeological Museum). Sixteenth century.

Church of St Vincent. Contains cart which carried lamb to shepherds' Midnight Mass. Twelfth century.

Chapel of White Penitents. Pastoral frescoes by popular painter, Yves Brayer.

Hôtel de Manville. Museum of modern art. Sixteenth century.

Protestant chapel. Sixteenth century.

Rue du Trencat. Hewn out of rock.

Bread ovens.

Hôtel de la Tour-de-Brau. Small lapidary museum; issues ticket for castle. Fourteenth century.

Chapels of St Claude and **St Blaise.** Fourteenth century.

Monument to local poet, Charloun Rieu of Paradou who wrote words for Noël at Midnight Mass (viewpoint).

Saracen Tower.

St Catherine's Chapel.

Paravelle Tower (view of castle).

Castle ruins and thirteenth-century keep (panoramic view).

Inscribed **Gallo-Roman votive stele.**

Stone pigeon-loft.

Montagnette hills overlooking the Rhône and Vallabrègue Dam. Boulbon is a pleasant old *bourg* whose focal point is its ruined castle. Each first of June they hold the Procession of the Bottles (*Fioles*) and blessing of the wine at the Chapel of St Marcellin, patron saint of wine.

Continue northwards on D81 and bear right on it to reach the Abbey of St Michel-de-Frigolet (from the Provençal word for thyme, for the building is set amidst aromatic herbs of the *garrigue*), immortalised in Alphonse Daudet's story, 'The Elixir of the Reverend Father Gaucher' from the *Lettres de mon moulin.*

The return to St Rémy is by Graveson, and Maillane which has been mentioned already as the place where Mistral was born and died.

Another itinerary west of St Rémy is by the N99, turning off at St Etienne-du-Grès on to the D32. At the next crossroads, and set back on the hillside on the left, is the curious twelfth-century chapel of St Gabriel. The Auberge du Carrefour has the key. A mixture of antique Roman motifs, Romanesque, Oriental and Classical themes cover the façade. By contrast, the interior is severely simple.

Tarascon Castle on the Rhône

Keep on the road signposted 'Fontvieille'. Outside the village is the Moulin de Daudet, a much-visited mill-museum because of its associations with Alphonse Daudet. The *Lettres de mon moulin* were not written here; Daudet did not write them entirely himself; he hardly ever visited the mill. He was essentially a Parisian teller of elegantly turned tales borrowed from Provençal sources.

Beyond the mill is a remarkable Roman ruin at Barbegal. A fourth-century water-mill was fed by ingenious aqueducts whose ruined arches can be seen not far away. Two parallel series of shutes worked sixteen water-mills which ground the local wheat for Arles and Rome. Slots which held the grindstones, and the course of the mill-race, are still visible.

Take the D82 towards Arles. 6km short of the town is the Abbey of Montmajour on rising ground above what had been marshland drained by the monks. Founded in the tenth century, it fell into a long decline and is now being restored. The keep is a powerful and commanding presence to contrast with the demure twelfth-century cloister and the church whose crypt is partly hewn out of the rock.

Do not miss the tiny burial chapel of Ste Croix in the form of a Greek cross in a field just below the abbey. It is a gem of Provençal Romanesque art, and is surrounded by tombs cut out of the rock.

An itinerary east of St Rémy allows a delightful part of the Alpilles to be discovered. Take the D5 south. For a panoramic view turn left after 4km and go to the top of La Caume (387m) for a sight of the flatlands of Crau, Camargue, lagoons, and the distant sea.

Continue on the D5 almost as far as Maussane where a left turn enters the peaceful valleys of the buckled, eroded

Alphonse Daudet's windmill, Fontvieille, contains Daudet Museum

flanks of the Alpilles. Follow the route Le Destet, Mas-de-Montfort, Aureille to Eyguières (and its fountains). Turn left on to the Orgon road (D569), and left again where the Castelas de Roquemartine ruins overlook the road. Return to Mas-de-Montfort, and turn right to Eygalières. Wander about it before continuing east to the twelfth-century chapel of St Sixte on a slope bare but for some cypresses, another of those unforgettable rural chapels. Hereabouts is Virgilian Provence.

The direct route back to St Rémy is by the D74A and N99, but the excursion can be extended by going from Eygalières to Orgon which has a vintage car museum (Musée Automobile).

For all the encroaching industrialisation, Martigues is still a name to conjure with from the days when artists (Augustus John, for

instance) fell in love with the little fishing port (and where the poet Roy Campbell briefly made his home). Martigues still has some old houses lining the canals.

Martigues is 53km from St Rémy, across the bleak and stony Grande Crau. Beyond Istres, left off the main road is ramparted St Mitre-les-Remparts, while St Blaise, a few kilometres in the opposite direction, is a site inhabited in the seventh century BC. A near-perfect Greek wall is the chief sight. Further south of Martigues are small fishing villages turned seaside resorts — Carro, Sausset-les-Pins, Carry-le-Rouet — in inlets at the foot of the arid Estaque range.

On the return journey a deviation can be made to Salon, olive-oil capital of Provence. Visit Château de l'Empéri for its displays of a history of the French

Army, its Nostradamus museum, and the regional Salon et Crau museum on the Pélissanne road.

The Camargue is a strange place. Flat, featureless, wind-swept, mosquito-ridden, flooded or else dried out, its luminous melancholy is captivating. Shallow, brackish lagoons, salt marshes

Montmajour Abbey near Arles: cloister and fortified tower. Founded by Benedictine monks who drained surrounding marshlands

Camargue: gardian *(cowboy) huts with blind and rounded north ends to break* mistral *wind*

and salt-tolerating plants, sand spits, coastal dunes, stunted tamarisks, small black bulls, and white horses, make southern Camargue a unique experience.

Coming from the direction of Arles, a quick impression can be gained by taking the D36, which follows the Grand Rhône for a while; turn right for Villeneuve; right again to skirt the north shore of the Nature Reserve of Etang de Vaccarès; pass rice paddies, vines and other crops in the desalinated area. Turn left on the N570 at Albaron towards Stes Maries-de-la-Mer.

Single-storeyed thatched cottages, blank on their north walls to keep out the *mistral,* the dwellings of the cowboys (*gardians*), are scattered about on the approaches to the only town of any size in the Camargue. Stes Maries is dominated by its fortress-church whose crypt contains the image of the black

Sarah, patron saint of gipsies.

Huge and colourful gipsy celebrations take place every 24-5 May, and again over the weekend nearest 22 October. The folklore and wildlife of the Camargue are explained in the Baroncelli Museum.

Take the secondary D38 north as far as Sylvéréal. Turn left on the D58 for Aigues-Mortes whose thirteenth-century ramparts and watch-towers are perfectly preserved. Steps lead to the top of the massive Tour Constance. Within the town, laid out in medieval grid pattern, the statue of Louis IX, St Louis, is a reminder that he set sail from Aigues-Mortes for the Seventh Crusade.

Grau-du-Roi is 6km away on the coast, a fishing village turned summer resort. From it, the ultra-modern resorts of La Grande-Motte and Port Camargue can be visited.

For a longer stay in the Camargue, numerous ranch-hotels offer guided riding holidays. There are also landrover tours, and boat trips along the Petit Rhône. At Méjanes is a holiday centre with a scenic railway, riding, mock bullfights in the arena, branding of young bulls (*ferrade*) and equestrian shows.

At Pont de Rousty, off N570 Albaron to Arles road, is the Musée Camarguais where the story of Camargue life is explained; walkers can follow a path into the marshes. Near Stes Maries, at

Ginès, is the Camargue Information Centre, from which is an advantageous view across the Etang de Vaccarès, the heart of the Camargue.

The Nature Reserve admits only accredited naturalists, but glimpses of birds, notably flamingoes (the only place in Europe where they breed regularly), are obtained by following the road which skirts the eastern side of Etang de Vaccarès, turns right at Le Paradis and leads to the causeway of the Gacholle lighthouse.

Well over 300 species of birds have

Interior of traditional gardian *(cowboy) hut in Camargue*

Méjanes, Camargue holiday centre: the train is only one of its attractions

Gipsy festival in May at Les Stes Maries-de-la-Mer, outside fortress-church

Aigues-Mortes, Canal du Rhône, part of waterway and irrigation systems to vitalise Provence's economy

Flamingoes in the Camargue, the most thrilling sight for bird-watchers

been recorded in the Camargue area. Little wonder that ornithologists come from the world over. For amateur and professional alike, the sight of massed flamingoes alighting, taking off, or standing on their raised nests, is the supreme delight. The appetite is whetted by the mention of a few characteristic birds: herons, storks, vultures, eagles, plovers, avocets, stilts, owls, bee-eaters, rollers, the carrying mating call of hoopoes, the exquisite nests of penduline tits . . . the list is only beginning.

4 Central Provence

Youthful vitality, as befits a university town, a character all its own, elegance inherited from its eighteenth-century past: these constitute some of the elements of Aix-en-Provence. Full of shops, hotels, restaurants and with much to see, it is a very attractive provincial city, an undisputed magnet.

Some people do not care to stay in large towns (and Aix has a population of 114,000); there are quieter places in the vicinity with agreeable hotels: Célony, Eguilles, Roquefavour, Beaureceuil, Vauvenargues, for instance. Yet a few days in the centre of Aix is a less tiring way of absorbing what it has to offer.

The old city, surrounded by boulevards from which radiate exits in all directions, exudes its seventeenth- and eighteenth-century personality, quite different from that of Avignon and Arles.

Begin with that aorta of Aix, the Cours Mirabeau, named after the scandalous and outstanding orator of the French Revolution, who ably represented Aix in the Paris parliament. It runs east and west. Planted in 1830 with four rows of plane trees, the Cours provides shade all summer long. Of its three fountains, the one at the eastern end is a statue of the fifteenth-century ruler of Provence, 'Good' King René (of Sicily, only a duke in Provence), scholar and patron of the arts and husbandry. He holds a bunch of muscat grapes, which he introduced (along with silkworms) into Provence. He may have been a politically incompetent ruler, but is viewed with affection in retrospect; his name is made use of by hotels, shops,

cafés and little businesses.

In the centre of Cours Mirabeau is the moss-covered Fontaine Chaude, coming from the same hot springs tapped by the Romans when they founded *Aquae Sextiae* in 122BC.

On the north side of the Cours are cafés, restaurants, bookshops and shops selling that speciality of Aix, *calissons,* delicate almond biscuits. On the south side are some seventeenth- and eighteenth-century mansions (*hôtels*) whose handsome doors, caryatids and wrought-ironwork characterise much of the old town.

Beyond Cours Mirabeau, to the north, as far as the cathedral, is Vieil Aix, the oldest part. Some of the streets are pedestrian thoroughfares; some are lined with smart shops selling antiques or Provençal handicrafts.

To obtain the flavour of Vieil Aix follow Rue Doumer from Cours Mirabeau. Turn right into Rue Espariat. At No 6, Hôtel Boyer d'Eguilles contains the Muséum d'Histoire Naturelle, with important collections of fishes and plants. Of more than passing interest is a unique display of dinosaurs' eggs, found embedded in Montagne Ste Victoire. Thousands of these eggs were unearthed. They had not hatched for several seasons. Was it a sudden cooling of the subtropical climate which caused six species of dinosaurs to become extinct, millions of years ago?

Rue Espariat leads into one of many little squares dotted about old Aix. This is Place d'Albertas, cobbled, with a fountain and terraced houses whose arches support the balconies of the

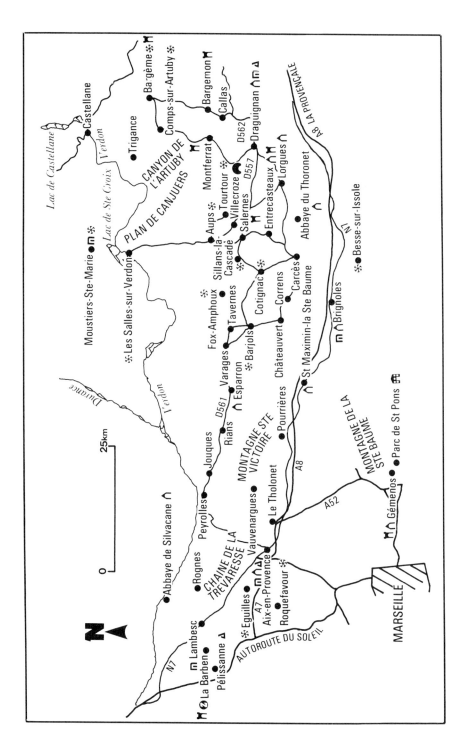

upper windows.

Turn right, across Places St Honoré and Verdun, past the Palais de Justice to Place des Prêcheurs (where the food market is held on Tuesday, Thursday and Saturday mornings). The front of Ste Marie-Madeleine church is uninteresting, but the interior has a masterly marble 'Virgin' by the Avignonnais J.P. Chastel (eighteenth century), and a fifteenth-century triptych of the 'Annunciation', full of mysterious symbols, perhaps painted by Jean Chapus. The church contains works by such well-known artists as J.B. and Carle van Loo, Nicolas Mignard, Michel Serre, and a 'Martyrdom of St Paul' attributed to Rubens.

If, instead, you turn left from Place d'Albertas, you come to Place Richelieu where a flower and vegetable market has been held for centuries. Poverty was said to have forced King René to sit at a stall and sell the produce of his own royal gardens.

The former Corn Market, now a sub-post office, was strikingly decorated by Chastel; the Rhône and Durance rivers are symbolised in the mythological figure of Cybele.

Adjoining is Place de l'Hôtel-de-Ville. Next to the town hall is a Flamboyant clock-tower of 1520. Below, modern statues (1925) represent Day and Night; above are wooden statuettes of the four seasons, each one visible for its three months. Higher still is the astronomical clock of 1661, and a Provençal bell-cage caps the tower.

The much rebuilt Hôtel-de-Ville contains the Méjanes Library (founded in 1787) of 300,000 books and manuscripts, an indispensable source of reference for scholars; also, the Fondation St John Perse, with memorabilia of this modern symbolist poet.

Turn right into Rue Gaston de Saporta (a nineteenth-century naturalist), once the Roman *Via Aurelia*, a street of elegant mansions and smart shops. Pierre Puget (1620-94) — Provence's greatest sculptor whose Baroque style was disliked by Louis XIV — is thought to have sculpted the façade of No 17, which houses the Musée du Vieil Aix. It is full of things which illuminate the arts and crafts of the past: faïences from Moustiers; documents relating to Mirabeau; old prints of Aix; nativity cribs (*santons*); old costumes and furniture; paintings on velvet. A few paintings by J.A. Constantin (1756-1844) are interesting because, even before John Constable, he painted from nature, a revolutionary practice.

Still further north is Place des Martyres-de-la-Résistance where the former Archbishop's Palace contains the Tapestry Museum, noted for eighteen Beauvais tapestries of the seventeenth and eighteenth centuries that include the *Life of Don Quixote*. During Aix's prestigious International Music Festival from mid-July to mid-August, the Palace courtyard serves as an open-air theatre.

In the Place de l'Université is the bust of Fabri de Peiresc (1580-1637), a Provençal universal savant.

Within the cathedral of St Sauveur are some of the oldest remains of Aix: the fifth-century baptistery supported by eight Roman columns covered by a sixteenth-century cupola. Part of the church began as the nave of a twelfth-century church (the cloisters, too, are of this period), later incorporated into the Gothic structure, a large part of which is sixteenth-century Flamboyant.

Find the sacristan to unlock where is kept the splendid triptych, 'The Burning Bush'. Painted by Nicolas Froment of Uzès in 1476, it shows King René kneeling on the left, portly, double-chinned and earthy compared with the religious figures in the panels. Also ask the sacristan to open the walnut panels of the West Door on which were carved the four prophets and twelve sybils in the sixteenth century. The south door leads to the Romanesque cloisters.

Although it lies just outside Vieil Aix, the Pavillon de Vendôme, 34 Rue Célony (close to the thermal baths), is a charming seventeenth-century house set in formal gardens. Built for Cardinal, Duke of Vendôme, it was later acquired by the influential Provençal painter, J.B. van Loo (1684-1745) — there were eleven artists in this family of Dutch origin — who died here. A handsome double staircase, period furniture and paintings sustain the original atmosphere.

Turn now to the south side of Cours Mirabeau, the once aristocratic Mazarin Quarter, smaller than Vieil Aix, the façades of its *Hôtels* more restrained.

Rue du 4 Septembre leads to Musée Paul Arbaud where are pictures by locally important artists, sculptures, ceramics and old furniture. Further along the street is one of Aix's most popular fountains, that of the Four Dolphins (1667). At right angles, in Rue Cardinale, is Lycée Mignet, the school attended by Paul Cézanne, Emile Zola and later the musician Darius Milhaud.

At the end of Rue Cardinale is the church of St Jean-de-Malte, the chapel to the former Priory of the Knights of St John of Malta, and the first Gothic church in Provence. Its interior is delightful for the purity of its proportions and the audacity of the lovely choir window. Its 67m-high belfry was built on the nave so that at street-level it is a chapel.

Almost next door is the former priory itself. In 1825 it was owned by the painter François Granet who willed it to the town of Aix with his collection; it has always been known as Musée Granet in preference to its formal title of Musé des Beaux-Arts.

Among the archaeological exhibits on the ground floor is a collection of Celto-Ligurian items removed from the *oppidum* of Entremont outside Aix. They pre-date all other pre-Roman sculptures known in France; primitive carvings of warriors' heads, death masks, a hand resting on the head whose eyes are closed, a bas-relief of a galloping horseman carrying a severed head on the neck of his mount.

There are galleries filled with paintings of many schools and periods, but take a closer look at the work of the Provençal *petits maîtres* whose interpretations of the landscapes around Aix give a profounder understanding of the contradictory elements in the countryside of Provence: J.A. Constantin, the earliest; François Granet (see also Ingres' sumptuous portrait of him), Prosper Grésy; particularly Paul Guigou, the finest Provençal landscapist before Cézanne, who created jewel-like colours and atmospheric depth; Emile Loubon, the pastoralist; Auguste Chabaud nearer our time.

Of Cézanne, there is virtually nothing. Aix awoke too late to his genius to afford anything of significance. The most intimate memento is his studio, preserved more or less as it was at his death. It is at 9 Avenue Paul Cézanne (in his day known as Chemin des Lauves), northwest beyond Boulevard Jean Jaurès. He had it built in 1902, the workshop of a man who in his art willed the landscape into the harmonious architectural planes and restrained colours which informed the paintings of his maturity and made him one of the

Cloister of St Sauveur, Aix-en-Provence

most significant figures in the history of art.

St Maximin-la-Ste Baume is 38km east of Aix along the N7. The basilica is the best example of Gothic architecture in Provence. Built on a sixth-century church, the basilica was started in 1295 as a resting-place, according to pious legend, for the remains of St Mary Magdalene (and later St Maximin). Intermittently worked on until the sixteenth century, no belfry was ever built, nor was the west front completed. Destined to be demolished during the French Revolution (when the town was renamed *Marathon*), good fortune found Napoleon's youngest brother Lucien — who called himself *Brutus* — turning the church into a storage depot. By having the 'Marseillaise' played regularly on the very organ in use today, he saved both building and contents.

Organ concerts of French music are given every summer, while the adjacent former Royal Monastery is a cultural centre which holds concerts each July.

Inside the austere and finely proportioned basilica can be seen the famous organ of 1773. Wooden panels — twenty-two in number — painted by the Venetian François Ronzen in the sixteenth century, include the earliest known view of the Palace of the Popes at Avignon. Choirstalls, screen, gilded statues and pulpit are all carved to a high standard.

La Ste Baume, with which the church of St Maximin is associated, is a mountain 23km south-west. The most venerable of Provençal legends insists that St Mary Magdalene lived in solitary retreat in a cave on La Ste Baume for the last thirty years of her life, having spent thirteen years with the Virgin Mary after Christ's crucifixion. Mary Magdelene, with St Maximin, the Virgin's sister Mary, Mary mother of James and John, various other saints of the Christian hagiolatry, plus the black servant Sarah, were cast adrift from the Holy Land in an open boat with neither sail nor oar, to land miraculously at Les Stes Maries-de-la-Mer. They parted and set about evangelising Provence. Maximin went to Aix to become its first bishop. Mary Magdalene made her way to La Ste Baume.

From the fifth century pilgrims streamed to the sacred place, until the Saracen invasions interrupted them. In the eleventh century the monks of Vézelay in Burgundy claimed to have acquired the saint's relics. Pilgrims went to Vézelay for five centuries. Then, St

Mary Magdalene's remains were discovered in the little Merovingian church at St Maximin. The basilica was erected; the pilgrims returned.

On Ste Baume, the cave (Grotte de St Pilon) can be reached on foot either from the one-time Hôtellerie (hostel) or the Carrefour des Chênes, both on the D80. Midnight Mass is celebrated on July 22. The panorama is impressive.

Nowhere is the contrast between the plant life of north and south slopes (in Provençal *hubacs* and *adrets* respectively) illustrated more clearly than in the Ste Baume range. South-facing slopes confront the full glare of heat and drought for which Mediterranean plants are adapted to survive. On the north, shaded and moist, is an extensive and remarkable forest. Beech, yew, maple, lime and privet — found hardly anywhere else in Provence — flourish in this grove once sacred to the Ligurians, and perhaps felled by Caesar as timber for his fleet. Royal decrees in the past and modern ideas on forest ecology have preserved the forest, a relic of distant times when the climate of Provence was more like that of Britain.

Take the winding descent of D2. On the left is Parc de St Pons whose trees, springs, waterfall, Romanesque chapel, ruined abbey, make a romantic parkland in which to roam.

At Gémenos, with its large eighteenth-century château, turn right and in about 2km, right again to come to the chapel of St Jean-de-Garguier. Its interest lies in the collection of some 200 *ex-voto* paintings done between 1500 and 1914. They are naive religious works, executed by anonymous local artists or artisans on behalf of people wishing to give thanks for divine interventions: for the safe delivery of a child, recovery from severe illness, or for any miraculous escape from death. *Ex-votos* hang in many a Provençal church, but those at St Jean-de-Garguier compress 400 years of gratitude for survival.

An attractive route running through the length of central Provence is the road between Aix and Draguignan. At first, the N96 northwards from Aix and then east as far as Peyrolles tends to be congested. The D561 branches right and runs peaceably in open, wooded countryside. It links the widely differing villages of Jouques, Rians, Esparron, Varages, Tavernes to Barjols (the latter having the largest plane tree in Provence, 12½m round its base; nearly the largest fountain; and a huge market-square).

A deviation south from Barjols by the D554, goes through Châteauvert and along the Vallon Sourn, a narrow valley enclosing the incipient river Argens, before the landscape opens out again at Correns, a quiet village, relatively untouched by tourism.

After Barjols is Cotignac. It is

PLACES TO VISIT FROM AIX

Entremont (3km north by Avenue Pasteur, D14). Ruins of religious and political capital of Saluvian Federation crushed by Romans, 123BC. Walls, towers, foundations of houses, temples. Fine views.

Roquefavour (12km west). Aqueduct (1842-7), much bigger than Pont du Gard. Ventabren by D64, ruined castle, views.

D17 north-west
Eguilles — Pélissanne ('Mur de Marius' Roman mausoleum) — La Barben (château, vivarium, zoo, miniature railway) — Lambesc — Abbaye de Silvacane (twelfth-century, restored, one of 'Three Sisters of Provence') — Rognes — Chaîne de la Trévaresse — Eguilles — Aix.

Circuit of Montagne Ste Victoire
D17 east — Le Tholonet — St Antoine-sur-Bayon — Puyloubier — Pourrières (said to be site of victory of Marius over Ambrones and Teutons in 102BC, luridly described in Plutarch's *Life of Marius*) — left D25 — left D223 — Vauvenargues (paths to Pic des Mouches, 1,011m and Croix de Provence, 969m) — D10 — Les Bonfillons (left for Barrage du Bimont reservoir with reflections of Ste Victoire, walk to Barrage Zola) — Aix.

picturesque and has a distinguished hotel, so that a day or two can be well spent here. An 80m-high brown cliff of tufa rock, riddled with one-time rock-shelters, rears behind the village.

From Cotignac a number of other charming villages repay a visit in these wide valleys where evergreen oaks dominate the woodlands: perched Fox-Amphoux; walled Sillans-la-Cascade's waterfall and Bresque stream where trout-fishermen meet; the thirteenth-century castle ruins at Salernes where tiles are made; Entrecasteaux, complete with a large château and gardens, Gothic fortified church, humpback bridge and medieval streets.

On higher ground is Villecroze and 5km away a waterfall and a cave — once fortified — whose petrified columns and fifteenth-century windows are still to be seen. Tourtour (633m), its restored honey-coloured stone houses, smart hotels, and two elm trees planted in 1638 to mark the birth of the future Sun King, Louis XIV, is a fashionable holiday centre with uninterrupted views over the Maures Mountains.

To the north is old Aups (stemming from the Celto-Ligurian *alb* 'hill pasture'), basking in a wide valley and backed by sheltering hills, whose honey has a local reputation.

Lorgues is a *bourg* with 4,500 inhabitants. Surrounded by vineyards and olive groves, its plane-filled square lends impressive dignity. A marble fountain, eighteenth-century church, and fourteenth-century fortified gateways all make a visit worthwhile.

2km west of Lorgues on the narrow D50 is a remarkable little chapel. It is the simple sixteenth-century Notre Dame de Benva (Bon Voyage), partly built into the rock. From its façade an arch spans the narrow path — once the main highway — and contemporary murals are clearly visible on the inner faces of the arch: Virgin and Child, St Joseph, St Christopher with the infant Jesus on his shoulder as he plunges a tree trunk into a stream. More murals

are within the chapel, but the door is almost invariably locked.

Brignoles, centre of bauxite-mining, marble-quarrying and wine production, 26km from Cotignac, justifies a visit to see in the Musée du Pays Brignolais what is thought to be the oldest of all Gaulish Christian sarcophogi. Of the third century, its carved messages are beautifully preserved; it was retrieved from the tiny chapel of La Gayolle, 10km west, on the estate of the St Julien farm.

After Brignoles, continue south of the N7 by the D554 and D15 for 21km to reach yet another intriguing village, Besse-sur-Issole. Just outside is one of the few natural lakes in Provence. Besse was the birthplace of Provence's eighteenth century Robin Hood, Gaspard de Besse. He spent a life of romanticised brigandage before he was caught and sentenced to be broken at the wheel by the judges of Aix. His execution was a social event attended by high-born ladies who wept at the young man's untimely death.

The third and finest Cistercian monastery of the 'three sisters of Provence' is the secluded abbey of Le Thoronet, 16km from Cotignac via Carcès. Set, like all Cistercian buildings, in a hollow to express the order's humility, the restored twelfth-century buildings of church, cloister, wash-house and chapter-house (simple carvings representing local flora are the only adornment), and dormitory are austere and harmonious.

Draguignan, with more than 26,000 inhabitants, is not normally thought of as a tourist centre, but as a place where the knowledgeable come to buy quality food at sensible prices.

Le Thoronet, finest of three Cistercian abbeys in Provence

There are modest but adequate hotels and restaurants; it makes a good excursion centre, and the old town is agreeable. Its heart is traffic-free and dominated by a seventeenth-century Tour d'Horloge. Streets and squares have evocative names: Place du Marché with its fountain; Rue des Marchands; Place aux Herbes and a medieval gateway; Rue des Tanneurs and the old Porte Aiguière; Rue de la Juiverie with the façade of a thirteenth-century synagogue.

A museum at 9 Rue de la République, in the eighteenth-century summer palace of the bishops of Fréjus, contains Gallo-Roman finds, coins, paintings, busts and natural history specimens, as well as some remarkable manuscripts in the large library.

Six rows of plane trees line the handsome Allées d'Azémar, flanked by gardens and mansions, and a bust of Georges Clemenceau who represented Draguignan in

North on D955 — left in 1km — prehistoric dolmen, Pierre de la Fée (three uprights supporting flat capstone) — deep Gorges de Châteaudouble and Nartuby river — village of Châteaudouble on edge of high cliff — Montferrat, ruined castle, Chapelle Notre Dame-de-Beauvoir — pass on left Plan de Canjuers (stark, rocky, pitted with underground caves, a military area barred to public) — valley of Artuby — Comps-sur-Artuby on rock spur, thirteenth-century church — Bargème (highest village in Var (1,094m) in castle ramparts) — footpath (6km) to ruins of Le Castellas overlooking Artuby gorge — Col du Bel-Homme (951m) — Bargemon (fountains, squares, old streets, castle, fortified gateways, church) — Callas — Draguignan.

Moustiers-Ste Marie, close to western end of Gorges du Verdon

Parliament for twenty-five years.

Europe cannot match Arizona's Grand Canyon, but the Verdon Gorges which borrow the name, Grand Canyon du Verdon, are nonetheless spectacular. The river is hemmed in by narrow cliffs which plunge 700m amid wild scenery. The Verdon gets its name from the green jade waters.

For 21km the river has gouged deeper in a geological fracture. Castellane or Trigance in the east, Moustiers-Ste Marie or Les Salles-sur-Verdon (a newish resort at the edge of the newish reservoir, Lac de Ste Croix) in the west, or from Comps-sur-Artuby or Aups: all offer approach roads to the river. All have hotel accommodation. Of them,

Castellane, a market-town as well as tourist centre and dominated by a cube of rock 180m high, has the largest number of hotel beds. It is also close to the inter-connected artificial lakes of Chaudanne, Castillon and St André-les-Alpes.

On both north and south sides of the gorge are memorable scenic roads provided with frequent stopping-places and belvederes. Drive with care along the winding, narrow roads which, here and there, are vertiginous.

THE VERDON GORGES

North route: Castellane — Moustiers - Ste Marie (45km)

D952 — Porte de St Jean defile — Clue de Chasteuil (narrow gorge) — Pont-de-Soleils — Clue de Carejuan — Point Sublime views — Route des Crêtes (fifteen belvederes, car parks) La Palud-sur-Verdon — valley of Maïre — Moustiers-Ste Marie.

South route: Moustiers-Ste-Marie — Castellane (82km)

D957 — Aiguines (seventeenth-century château) — Col d'Illoire (964m) — Cirque de Vaumale (highpoint, 1,204m) — views along Corniche Sublime — two tunnels —

Pont de l'Artuby (single span of 110m over Artuby gorge) — Balcons de Mescla ('watersmeet') — Comps-sur-Artuby — Pont-de-Soleils — Castellane.

Walking

Footpath (GR4 Sentier Martel) between Chalet La Maline to Point Sublime (15km). White and red arrows. Allow 8 hours. Stout shoes, warm clothing, food and drink, torch (some tunnels). Taxi for return journey at Point Sublime. Recommended summer months only.

Exploration of gorge bottom on foot or kayak for specialists only.

5 Western Riviera: Marseille to Fréjus

The French Riviera — the most renowned of all coasts — is the subject of this and the next chapter. Visions of sea and beaches spring to mind, so a few general comments about both may take precedence over discussions about town and countryside.

Cliffs, rocks, inlets, small bays, ribbons of sand, pebble beaches: all these help make up the coast's profile. There is no need to detail the facilities offered by each resort. On many public beaches are areas (*plages aménagés*) where concessionnaires provide

---

MAIN SANDY BEACHES BETWEEN
MARSEILLE AND FREJUS

La Ciotat-Plage (3km north-east of La Ciotat, in curving bay)

Les Lecques (over 1km long in bay between Les Lecques and La Madrague, safe)

Hyères-Plage (6km south of Hyères, sheltered, shallow, warm, backed by umbrella pines)

La Capte (9km south of Hyères on Giens Peninsula; 3km long backed by pines)

Le Pellegrin and **L'Estagnol** (7 and 8km south-east of La Londe-les-Maures in Bay of Hyères; almost unspoiled, shallow, safe; private, admission charges)

Cabasson (curved bay, shallow)

Le Lavandou (2km long, car parking on promenade)

St Clair (east facing bay, car parking on promenade)

Cavalière (sheltered, backed by pines; one of finest beaches of Maures coast)

Pramousquier and **Canadel-sur-Mer** (small but safe, sheltered)

Cavalaire (3km of safe sands north of resort)

Gigaro (5km south-east of La Croix-Valmer; secluded)

St Tropez (6km unbroken sands between Plage de Tahiti and south end of Plage de Pampelonne; some private, a few public)

Ste Maxime (2km safe, south-facing sands; shady promenade)

St Aygulf (long, gently shelving; pine forest)

Fréjus-Plage (1½km south of Fréjus, extensive, almost joined to St Raphaël)

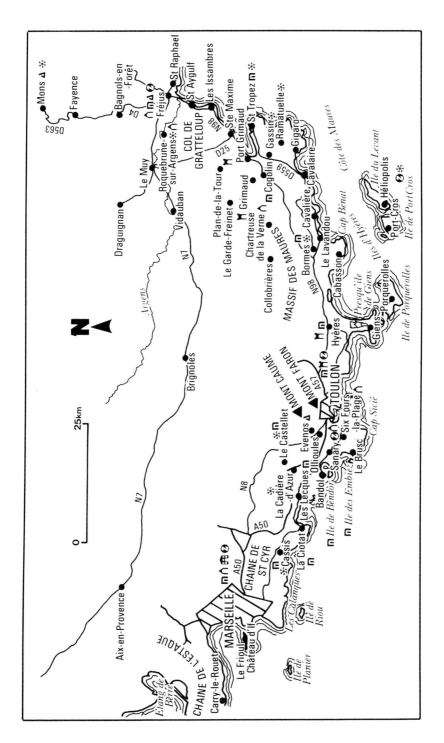

La Bourse, Marseille, houses Maritime Museum and Library. Seat of oldest Chamber of Commerce in France (1599). Foreground: statue in honour of Pierre Puget, greatest Provençal sculptor

refreshments, hire beach equipment (sunshades, sunbeds, etc), sail-boards and pedaloes, and perhaps there are swimming and wind-surfing instructors. Larger resorts have many ancillary recreational facilities, such as yachting and water-skiing, while there are subaqua and marine archaeological clubs for specialists.

A nearly land-locked sea produces an inter-tidal zone measured in centimetres; the width of beach varies imperceptibly. Intense evaporation creates high salinity and a buoyancy for swimmer and physically handicapped people alike. The famous intense Mediterranean blue

Cavalière

Port Grimaud

Ascending Col d' Allos

— a delight to the eye — indicates a paucity of planktonic life.

Pressure in this very deep sea creates a constant annual temperature of 13°C and gives a thermostatic effect; the coast is warmed in winter and cooled in summer. As these figures show, inshore water is slow to cool in autumn.

Mean sea temperatures in °C

	Marseille-Toulon	Toulon-Menton
May	15	16
Jun	20	19
Jul	19	21
Aug	21	23
Sep	17	23
Oct	18	19

However, such statistics are a little deceptive. The *mistral* can play havoc with surface temperatures, especially between Marseille and St Tropez. It may not blow for long in summer, but the water is made chill and rough (particularly along west-facing beaches), but as the water calms, the sun's heat quickly raises the water temperature about 3°C to make the difference between brave and comfortable swimming.

For most of the year French time is an hour ahead of that in Britain. As sunset is earlier in the south, and the dusk is brief, the extra hour is an evening bonus in early summer and autumn.

Marseille, the major port of the Mediterranean and the oldest town in France, is an expanding commercial, industrial and university city. Volatile, energetic, raw-humoured, chaotic at rush-hours, its Levantine origins seem never to be far from the surface. Its endearing character was affectionately portrayed by the popular and ebullient

Marseille, imposing Baroque Palais Longchamp containing Fine Arts and Natural History Museums

97

Santons, *traditional clay figurines in early nineteenth-century Provençal costumes*

WHAT TO SEE IN MARSEILLE
(In addition to places listed under Further Information)

Modern **port installations of La Joliette** (Sunday and public holidays only: on foot from Arenc gate).

Unité d'Habitation, Boulevard Michelet: seventeen-storey dwelling unit on stilts, built 1952 by Le Corbusier.

Basilica of Notre Dame-de-la-Garde: panoramic views.

Parc du Pharo: fine views.

Shopping: smart shops of Rue de Rome, Rue St Férréol; indoor shopping area, Centre Bourse.

Picturesque quarter: Le Panier, between Place de Lenche, La Major Cathedral and Rue de la République.

Fish market: Vieux Port (Mon-Sat am).

Santons Fair: last fortnight in Dec, La Canebière: sale of traditional painted clay figurines in early nineteenth-century costumes.

Botanic Garden, Parc Borély.

Vieux Port: buildings, harbour, yachts.

EXCURSIONS BY BOAT

(Information from Office de Tourisme)

Two ferries cross Vieux Port between Quai du Port and Quai de Rive Neuve.

Château d'If: all year, round trip (90 minutes) from Quai des Belges, Vieux Port. Once fortress/prison for thousands of prisoners (and fictional *Count of Monte Cristo* by Alexandre Dumas) on islet; fine views of Marseille.

Ile Frioul (sailing and sports centre); **Ile de Planier** (lighthouse); **Ile Riou** (interesting for naturalists: racial variety of wall lizard; species of gecko unknown on mainland; only Provençal habitat of peregrine falcon).

Longer tours to **Etang de Berre** and **Martigues.**

Motor launches to *calanques* of **Sormiou, Morgiou** and **Sugiton** (also accessible on foot from Centre Universitaire, Luminy, south-east Marseille).

Cassis, La Ciotat and *calanques.*

Two-day cruises to **Iles d'Hyères.**

Château d'If, favourite excursion by boat from Vieux Port, Marseille

Calanque *(fjord) of Port-Miou near Cassis*

---

actor Fernandel (1903-71). Marseille is
certainly stimulating. A car is only an
encumbrance; use the city and suburban
buses, trolley-buses, taxis or the
underground (Métro) service.

Of hotels there is no shortage:
impersonal, international hotels; a few

elegant converted residences; adequate
modest places, either in the centre of the
city or along the Corniche Président
Kennedy. Restaurants range equally
widely; some have a *Michelin* rosette.
Many will offer Marseille's august dish,
bouillabaisse, that superb fish stew and

soup for which everybody claims to have the only authentic recipe. If it is genuine, it must be expensive. Michel, 6 Rue des Catalans, arguably provides the best *bouillabaisse,* as well as that other Provençal delicacy *bourride* (a creamy fish soup).

La Canebière (from *chènevière,* hempfield) was originally the rope-makers' street, and is now the boulevard of departure and return for the visitor. Apart from its shops, cafés and bars, the Tourist Office is at No 4 near the Vieux Port.

On the road from Marseille to Cassis stop at Col de la Gineste. Inland is a view of the denuded white limestone Chaîne de St Cyr. Seawards is the inlet of Cassis, and beyond, the towering Cap Canaille, the highest cliff in France (399m). Sometimes, of a September evening, the panorama is suffused with intense purple light.

Cassis is a cheerful, busy little port, visited in numbers by the Marseillais. It has a recent (1977) casino and holds regattas and water-sports events in summer. Deep, fjord-like inlets of sheer limestone to the west of Cassis — the *calanques* of Port-Miou, Port-Pin and En-Vau — are best seen close to by boat excursion from Quai St Pierre. Port-Miou is accessible by car, and from its car park follow the footpath. The *calanques* are a test of the rock-climber's skill.

In the opposite direction from Cassis is the *Corniche des Crêtes,* over Pas de la Colle and Cap Canaille and on to the naval dockyard of La Ciotat.

Beyond is Les Lecques whose good sandy beach makes it popular. At La Madrague is the Tauroentum Museum with Gallo-Roman mosaics and relics, built on the foundations of a Roman villa near the sea.

Bandol, one of the more sophisticated coastal resorts, has bars and discos, and a Jardin Exotique et Parc Zoologique, 3km north-east of the town. Pleasant grounds laid out with exotic trees give shelter to a variety of small animals and birds. The whole hinterland is attractive for touring; go and see the villages of La Cadière-d'Azur and Le Castellet. Just off the N8 is the Ricard motor race-track and car museum; also on the N8 is the OK Corral amusement park.

Off-shore is Ile de Bendor to which motor-boats ply frequently from Bandol. Not many years ago it was an empty rock, now an imitation Provençal fishing port and artisanal village have appeared. An art gallery, open-air theatre, zoo, the remarkable World Museum of Wines and Spirits, a nautical club, hotels and restaurants attract many visitors.

Next comes Sanary, popular with yachtspeople. On the further side of the A50 autoroute is the Jardin Exotique Sanary-Bandol containing birds, monkeys, and exotic plants in glasshouses.

Take the road from Sanary to Le Brusc. A short way out to sea is the Ile des Embiez which has become well known through the marine research work conducted there by the biologist Alain Bombard and funded by Paul Ricard's Fondation Océanographique. As well as an aquarium and museum, the island has a marina, shipyards and hotel. From Le Brusc make for Notre Dame du Mai (1625) the high point of Cap Sicié (358m) and commanding extensive views, before returning via Six-Fours-la-Plage.

Like Marseille, the great naval base of Toulon is not usually visualised as a holiday centre, but it holds things of interest in addition to its dramatic setting at the foot of Mont Faron and, further away, Mont Caume, both surmounted by forts.

Toulon: téléphérique to Mont Faron

Make a point of seeing the Musée Naval. Two powerful caryatids, *Force* and *Fatigue* stand at the entrance, the work of Pierre Puget in 1656, master sculptor at Toulon dockyard during the reign of Louis XIV. Many of Puget's drawings of ships are in the museum.

The Musée d'Art et d'Archéologie has Gallo-Roman and oriental exhibits and worthwhile paintings by Provençal artists such as Guigou, Monticelli, Engalière, van Loo, as well as more modern works by Vlaminck and others.

Part of the old town, miraculously escaping the Allied bombing of the port, is a pedestrian zone of considerable charm. In July and August they hold a circus performers' festival. A covered fish market and a vegetable and flower market give further animation each morning.

From Quai Stalingrad motor-boat trips go round the inner roadstead (Petite Rade) to include the arsenal and dry docks. Les Sablettes and St Mandrier and the Iles d'Hyères make short boat excursions; Corsica can be visited between June and September.

18km east of Toulon lies Hyères, the oldest resort of the Riviera. First admired in the sixteenth century by Catherine de Medici who thought of building a royal villa at Hyères, and patronised three centuries later by Queen Victoria and R.L. Stevenson, its exposed position in winter made it fall out of favour. It lies between the limestone ranges to the west and the Maures mountains to the east.

Stroll about the old town, huddled round the hilltop castle ruins. A medieval flavour hangs about the streets, particularly Rue Paradis and Place Massillon where markets are held on weekdays. Broad avenues lined with palms give the new town a sub-tropical look. The Municipal Museum is of interest by virtue of the Greek and Roman finds from the Greek settlement of *Olbia,* today's l'Almanarre which is itself descended from an Arab word *Al Manar* (lighthouse), and Saracen pottery has been found there.

The beaches are further south, close to the neck of a 7km-long peninsula, the Presqu'île de Giens, on whose west side are the Pesquier saltmarshes and a lagoon. At the tip is Tour Fondue from which boats take 15 minutes to reach the island of Porquerolles. Other departures are from Cavalaire, Port de la Plage d'Hyères and Le Lavandou; these crossings take much longer.

Porquerolles (*Prote* or 'first' to the Greeks) is the largest of the group of islands known as the Iles d'Hyères or, more romantically, Les Iles d'Or, the

Golden Isles. From the minuscule port of Porquerolles (where bicycles can be hired) paths go in various directions through lush vegetation and vineyards.

Port Cros (motor-boats take 90 minutes from Port de la Plage d'Hyères), called *Mese* or 'middle' by the Greeks, is more rugged than Porquerolles. The whole of the tranquil, hilly island is a nature reserve which includes the sea fringe. Botanical rambles and underwater viewing of marine life are escorted by guides, and useful booklets explaining the island's natural history can be bought.

The third island, Ile du Levant, is reached from Le Lavandou and Cavalaire. Most of it is occupied by the French navy; only the western tip and the nudist village of Heliopolis can be visited.

East of Hyères begins the Côte des Maures, the 'new' Riviera, discovered as a summer pleasure-ground in the inter-war years. Backing the coast is the Massif des Maures (from the Greek *amauros* and Provençal *maouro,* 'sombre' in reference to the sombre colour of the pine trees). Some 60km long between Hyères and Fréjus, its hills, rounded by erosion, are thickly forested with pines (prone to forest fires), cork-oaks and Spanish chestnuts. The crystalline rock contains mica-schist which glints like gold in the sun.

After crossing the neck of Cap Bénat to Le Lavandou, the coastal road out of Hyères links a chaplet of small resorts, each with its individual character: St Clair, La Fossette, Aiguebelle, Cavalière, Pramousquier, Canadel, Rayol, Cavalaire and, crossing the promotory of Ramatuelle, St Tropez. Sandy beaches and coves predominate; on these beaches the Allied armies landed in 1944 to begin the liberation of Provence. All these resorts virtually close down at the end of September.

Once the yachts, aspirants to stardom or notoriety, nudes and the crowds who want to share in the dream-world have left, St Tropez reveals itself as endearingly attractive as when Matisse painted it long ago. Derain, Braque, Marquet, Bonnard, Dufy and a host of other artists fell under the spell of the white light and immortalised St Tropez in paint, as did Colette in literature.

The work of some of these turn-of-the-century masters is housed in the Museum of Modern Art, Place Georges Grammont (the benefactor). Not only is the exhibition a delight, the building also is pleasing to look at. The other museum in the town is the Maritime Museum in the Citadel; among many other exhibits are engravings of old St Tropez.

Two venerable processions take place every year in St Tropez. They are the *bravades* (literally, 'bravados'). One takes place between 16 and 18 May. The gilded bust of St Torpes is carried round the town by a corps of a hundred *bravadeurs* dressed in eighteenth-century costume who make a prodigious noise with muskets, blank cartridges and music. Bystanders join in the fun. On the last day, the procession makes its way to the pretty sixteenth-century chapel of Ste Anne on a rock just south of the town. The ritual celebrates the arrival in an open boat of the body of the martyred Christian centurion of Pisa.

The second *bravade* is on 15 June. The *Fête des Espagnols* honours the putting to flight of the Spanish fleet by valiant *Tropéziens* in 1637 during the Thirty Years' War.

On the quay is the statue of the Bailli de Suffren (1729-88), the admiral who, with only five ships under his command, harrassed the English fleets from the West Indies to the Indian Ocean. Château Suffren, the family home, is in the old town, near the town hall.

In summer frequent motor-boat excursions round the Gulf of St Tropez, and further afield, can be taken.

After St Tropez it would be a pity not to see Port Grimaud. Leave the car at the entrance to the village, for Port Grimaud can be visited only on foot or by boat. It is an elegant modern holiday village built out into the Gulf of St Tropez, and designed with the yachting community in mind; each front door has its own mooring. It is an imitation Provençal fishing village with harmonious colours, and graceful

Port Grimaud, elegant modern holiday village using traditional maritime Provençal style

bridges over canals from one walkway to another. Shops, banks, cafés, church and post-office are grouped around a beflowered square. Self-drive boats can be hired to tour the canals, or there are sightseeing cruises.

Ste Maxime, with a population approaching 7,000, is a lively resort sheltered, unlike St Tropez across the bay, from the *mistral*. Fine beaches — especially at La Nartelle — entertainment at night, a 9-hole golf course at Beauvallon, and plenty of hotels and restaurants (some remain open in winter), makes Ste Maxime popular. From it, the D25 leads inland towards Le Muy and Draguignan. Side roads, especially those between Col de Gratteloup on the D25, Plan-de-la-Tour and Vidauban on N7 provide quiet round trips among the lower Maures hills.

The road (N98) still follows the coast. Cap des Sardinaux is yet another stopping-place for exhilarating views. Tiny resorts are hidden among trees: Val d'Esquières, San Peire-sur-Mer, Les Issambres, and St Aygulf, widely known for its excellent camping facilities, which is separated from Fréjus-Plage by the mouth of the river Argens.

Fréjus-Plage has extensive sands which are 1½km southeast of the town of Fréjus. Fréjus is far enough inland not to be a resort, and its chief attractions are its Roman and medieval past.

Guided tours of episcopal Fréjus, which is concentrated at Place Formigé in the town's centre, are organised throughout the year by the *Syndicat d'Initiative* in Place Calvini.

An austere early Provençal Gothic cathedral of the thirteenth century is on the right. As you enter, you see that it is powerful rather than graceful (Provençal architects had not yet mastered the

subtlety of Gothic art). Make a point of seeing a retable on wood by the Nice painter Jacques Durandi (1450), and the chancel choirstalls of the fifteenth century.

Close by is a fifth-century baptistry, octagonal within, and one of the oldest in France.

In the same group of buildings are the restored twelfth-century cloisters. A garden and ancient well are surrounded by delicate, twin-columned marble

PLACES OF INTEREST AROUND FREJUS

Buddhist pagoda (3km north-east on N7): shrine to dead Indo-Chinese soldiers of 1914-18 War, next to cemetery of 5,000 Annamite graves.

Chapelle de Notre Dame de Jérusalem (in grounds of La Tour de Mare estate, 3km beyond pagoda, off right from N7): modern chapel decorated in 1963 with designs by Jean Cocteau.

Safari de l'Esterel (D4 north for 3½km, right): wild animals at liberty, viewed from closed car windows.

Parc Zoologique (near Safari de l'Esterel): animals and birds in open.

Valley of Argens, **Roquebrune-sur-Argens**: picturesque, arcaded houses, Convent of Notre Dame de Pitié (views); walk to Montagne de Roquebrune (372m) and Notre Dame de la Roquette chapel.

Scenic run through Bagnols-en-Forêt and Fayence to **Mons** (804m) high over Siagnole and Siagne valleys; Roman aqueduct (*Roche Tailée*).

pillars; the beams of the arcades were painted in the fourteenth and fifteenth centuries with innumerable creatures and grotesques illustrating the Apocalypse. Adjoining the cloisters is the Archaeological Museum consisting largely of finds from excavations of Roman Fréjus.

Fréjus, 2,000 years ago, was on the sea, and here Julius Caesar created a trading post, *Forum Julii*, on the Aurelian Way in 49BC. A little later, Octavius, the future Emperor Augustus, developed the place into a major naval base and settlement for his retired soldiers. For 200 years the large harbour was kept skilfully dredged. Then its importance diminished, the river Argens silted up the harbour, and Fréjus became surrounded by malarial marshes.

While the mind's eye may be able to reconstruct the layout of *Forum Julii* from the widely scattered remnants about the modern town, they are disappointing, with the exception of the arena. To visit the latter, park the car in Place Agricola, Rue Général de Gaulle. Fragments of Roman wall support the terrace of the *place,* and one tower of the Porte des Gaules survives, as does a small paved section of *Via Aurelia.* The arena, the oldest in Gaul, is 300m west along Rue Henri Vadon. Its dilapidation through centuries of pillage was hastened by Roman jerry-building and cheese-paring on the budget; there was none of the refinement lavished on other buildings in Roman Provence. The seating has been restored and bullfights and concerts are held in the amphitheatre in summer.

Keen students of the past will seek out the traces of the only surviving example in France of a Roman naval and civil base: small theatre, aqueduct, citadel (the *Plate-Forme*), Porte d'Italie, Porte d'Orée (the arch attached to the baths), laundry, and the Lanterne d'Auguste (a medieval harbour landmark built on the foundations of a Roman lighthouse). The railway line runs over what was the 54-acre harbour.

The simple life on the edge of the Mediterranean at Le Dramont

6 Côtes d'Azur:
St Raphaël to Menton___

A writer thought up the name 'Côte
d'Azur' in 1887 for the French Riviera
between Cannes and Menton. For the
sake of convenience I include the coast
between St Raphaël and La Napoule
which strictly should be known as the
Côte de l'Esterel.

The Esterel is an ancient and eroded
range whose highest point is Mont
Vinaigre (628m). Jagged, rust-red rocks
of volcanic porphyry rise dramatically
behind the coast, sending out
breakwaters of red rocks into the
emerald and ultramarine sea. This is the
most colourful part of the Riviera coast.
Less wooded than the Maures — but as
much a prey to forest fires — there are
areas of dense shrubby undergrowth, the
maquis.

The most attractive parts are reached
on foot from the small coastal resorts of
Agay, Anthéor and Le Trayas on the
N98 (the *Corniche d'Or*): the peaks of
Mont Vinaigre, Pic d'Aurelle, Pic du
Cap Roux, Col des Lentisques and the
narrow valley of Mal-Infernet. By car,
the N7 skirts the north side of the Esterel
for twenty-eight winding kilometres.

St Raphaël (24,400 inhabitants) — its
sedate air attracts the epithet 'the
Bournemouth of the Riviera' — has a
marina, casino and extensive beaches
extending to the smart suburb of
Boulouris. Scuba-divers have filled the
Museum of Underwater Archaeology,
Rue des Templiers, with amphorae and
other finds, and techniques of
underwater archaeology are also on
show. Next door is the twelfth-century
Templars' fortress-church which
defended the populace from maritime

marauders.

Between St Raphaël and La Napoule
lie small resorts — Boulouris, Agay,
Anthéor, Le Trayas, Miramar, La
Galère, Théoule — tucked into little
bays at the foot of the Esterel, some
rocky, some sandy. Beyond Anthéor the
Côte de l'Esterel reveals its most
impressive scenery; the road skirts the
bold mass of Cap Roux (452m), and
near Le Trayas rocks, pines and sea
unite to an intensity of colour.

La Napoule, with three beaches,
marina and 18-hole golf course, as well
as a massive medieval castle, is at the
eastern end of the Esterel range, and is
the gateway to the Côte d'Azur proper.

The gently folded east-west ranges
which give Provence its 'classical'
harmonies begin to be replaced by
narrow alpine valleys running north and
south which culminate in 3,000m peaks
in the north of the Alpes-Maritimes.
These mountain formations protect the
coast. Places like Beaulieu (often
referred to as *'Petite Afrique'*) and
Menton (where the average winter
temperature is 9.6°C) experience fog, ice
or snow as sensational rarities.

The same mountains confine the
warmth, voluptuous colours and exotic
plants to a coastal ribband.
Paradoxically, most of the eye-catching
trees, shrubs and flowers are imported:
Bougainvillea, prickly pear, loquat,
mimosa, bananas, oranges, lemons and
many other varieties of citrus fruits,
begonias, palms, aloe, agave,
mesembryanthemum. Even the olive
tree, which attains its most majestic
proportions here, is not strictly

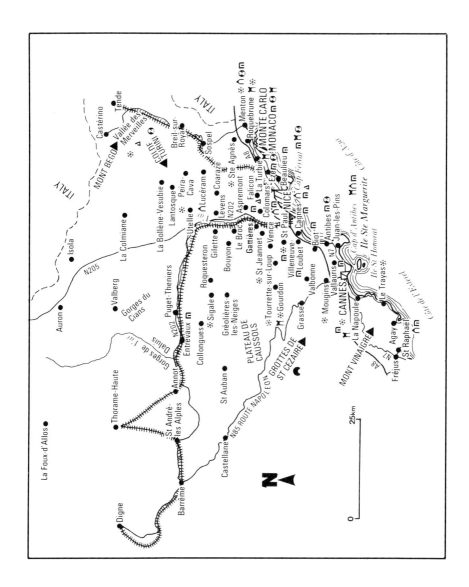

indigenous; it was probably planted by the Greeks in the sixth century BC.

A cultural difference between the Côte d'Azur and Provence is noticed. The former is Italianate, reflecting the long periods during which the County of Nice was part of Italy. Whole streets and squares in Menton, Nice and Villefranche are architecturally Italian.

The traditional Nissard cuisine is orientated towards Italy. Italian-sounding surnames abound.

At no great distance inland, the altitude rises quickly and the landscape becomes alpine; the only thing it seems to have in common with the Mediterranean is a limpid light. In winter or spring you can bask in warm coastal sunshine, and ski in an hour or so on the deep soft snows at Peïra-Cava, Col de Turini, Gréolières-les-Neiges, La Colmiane, La Foux d'Allos, or at the three major resorts of the Alpes-Maritimes, Valberg, Auron and Isola 2000 which have extensive *pistes,* lifts, ski schools and equipment for hire.

This rapid and dramatic contrast between coast and hinterland lends exhilaration to an exploration of the region in summer and winter.

Densely populated, the Côte d'Azur is almost a conurbation between Cannes and Menton. Driving and parking present familiar difficulties. There are other ways of getting about than by car. Flights between Britain and busy Nice-Côte d'Azur Airport (on the eastern tip of the Var estuary) are frequent. Coaches and taxis connect with Nice and the other resorts.

French Railways (SNCF) run overnight services from Calais and Paris to most of the major resorts between Marseille and Menton. Between May and September local half-hourly tourist trains (*Métrazur*) link all stations between St Raphaël and Menton.

Two very worthwhile railway excursions can be made from Nice. One starts from the Gare Centrale to go through the mountain scenery by way of Peille, Sospel, Breil-sur-Roya to Tende, and takes something over two hours.

The second itinerary is the justly famous autorail scenic journey by the Chemins de Fer de la Provence from Gare de Provence in Nice, Place de la Libération. It takes in the valleys of the Var, Vaïre, Verdon and Asse, to the stations of Puget-Theniers, Entrevaux, Annot, Thorame-Haute, St André-les-Alpes to Digne (151km). It takes 3hr

Peillon, one of many dramatic perched villages along Côte d'Azur

Pégomas: Hôtel Le Bosquet; 17 rooms plus 7 studios with kitchenettes (no restaurant). Tel: (93) 42 22 87

Mougins: Hôtel France; 8 rooms. Tel: (93) 90 00 01

Valbonne: Auberge Fleurie; 10 rooms. Tel: (93) 42 02 80

La Colle-sur-Loup: Marc Hély; 13 rooms. Tel: (93) 22 64 10

St Paul: Le Hameau; 16 rooms (no restaurant). Tel: (93) 32 80 24

Vence: Les Muscadelles, Avenue H. Giraud; 14 rooms. Tel: (93) 58 01 25

Colomars: Hôtel Rédier; 26 rooms. Tel: (93) 08 11 36

Peillon: Auberge de la Madone; 18 rooms. Tel: (93) 79 91 17

Peille: Auberge du Seuillet; 7 rooms. Tel: (93) 41 17 39

Monti: Pierrot-Pierrette; 3 rooms. Tel: (93) 35 79 76

20min in each direction; the return can be made on the same day.

SNCF also run coach excursions, some as far afield as Grenoble and Geneva over the spectacular Route des Alpes. A booklet of rail and coach services is obtainable from railway stations and Tourist Offices.

Regular coach services between Nice and Marseille (200km), daily in season, are operated by Phocéen-Cars. During the summer you can cruise along the Riviera coast from Lido-Plage, Promenade des Anglais, Nice.

To see something of the coastal resorts while not actually staying in them, consider staying at a rural hotel a little inland. A few agreeable and reasonably priced hotels are suggested.

Coming from La Napoule, you reach Cannes. Le Suquet tower in the old town is the beacon which identifies Cannes from a distance. On the west side is the port, the Municipal Casino (open November-May) and the old town on gently rising ground. To the east are the sandy beaches and the glittering Boulevard de la Croisette with hotels, shops, cafés and marinas. On the Pointe de la Croisette is the Palm-Beach Casino (June-October) with restaurant, cabaret, disco and swimming-pool under the same roof. Find Rue d'Antibes for smart shops and discos. In Rue des Belges is the Casino des Fleurs; Rue Meynadier has food shops; morning markets are held in Rue Louis Blanc.

On the heights is the Observatory at La Californie; lifts take you to the top of the tower for one of the finest coastal views in Europe. See the sun setting behind the Esterel and you will see why Kipling said this was the most beautiful coast in the world.

Boats go to the Iles de Lérins (Ile Ste Marguerite in 15min, Ile St Honorat, 30min). Sightseeing of the historical buildings on the two islands combines with woodland walks to make this an attractive half-day excursion.

Juan-les-Pins started life in the 1920s, has no history, but is blessed with fine sands. Its noisy night-life falls silent at

Cannes, port and old part of Le Suquet

the end of the season.

By contrast, walk along the sea walls of Antibes and about the old town's narrow and bustling streets. The Picasso Museum in Château Grimaldi is understandingly laid out in a handsome

building and does justice to the diversity of the genius who spent much of his long life (1881-1973) in the South of France.

Take the D2559 for a tour round the peninsula of Cap d'Antibes, still the elegant preserve of estates which

of sailors' ex-votos. Mementoes connected with Napoleon's return from Elba are shown in the Musée Naval et Napoléonien, and the coastal views from this point are delightful.

La Brague, outside Antibes, has a beach with lido, water-sports, nightlife with bars and dancing, and casino. Nearby is a favourite family attraction, Marineland with zoo, aquarium and performing animals.

Biot, inland on the D4 from La Brague, is surrounded by acres of carnations and roses for the Riviera flower markets. The ubiquitous and handsome terra-cotta vases that adorn many gardens once formed the main industry of Biot.

Outside the village is the Fernand Léger Museum. Its huge, garish mosaic façade looks out of place in this setting. Works by this robust northern artist (1881-1955), interpreter-in-chief of the factory age, fill the museum built by his widow.

Cagnes-sur-Mer is a sprawling mass which has engulfed the chic race-course, l'Hippodrome de la Côte d'Azur. In Cagnes-Ville is the Renoir Museum, Avenue des Collettes, the house and garden where Renoir (1841-1919) spent the last twelve years of his pain-racked life. You have the impression that everything has been left much as it was: the tools of his trade in the studio, a painting, some drawings and sculptings — including his bronze *Venus* in the garden surrounded by ancient olive trees — correspondence, photos, mementoes. The whole is a moving tribute to an artist who expressed his love of the freshness of life.

At Haut-de-Cagnes, the prettiest part of Cagnes, the handsome Château-Musée houses an exhibition devoted to the olive tree, that veritable symbol of Provence. Also in the château is a

cultivate exotic flora. Jardin Thuret, owned by the State and open to the public, was one of the first gardens to acclimatise tropical trees and plants. Visit also the chapel of La Garoupe, next to the lighthouse, for its collection

Ile St Honorat, reached by boat from Cannes

<table>
<tr><td colspan="2">PLACES OF INTEREST ROUND CANNES</td></tr>
<tr><td>Tanneron Hills (mimosa in January) and Lake St Cassien (sailing, swimming, wind-surfing).</td><td>Sophia-Antipolis (modern international scientific park research buildings).</td></tr>
<tr><td>Grottes de St Cézaire (illuminated caves).</td><td>Mougins (fashionable, charming hill-village).</td></tr>
<tr><td>Grasse (terraced promenade of Cours Honoré-Cresp; ex-cathedral and paintings; perfumeries; Villa-Musée Fragonard and work by J.H. Fragonard; Provençal Art and History Museum).</td><td>Gorges du Loup (scenery; waterfall).

Gourdon ('eagle's nest' perched village).

Le Bar (Bréa altarpiece in church).</td></tr>
<tr><td>Vallauris (Madoura Pottery Works; Picasso Museum of his War and Peace mural; Picasso bronze Man and Sheep).</td><td>Tourette-sur-Loup (site and views).

Route Napoléon (N85) towards Castellane (upland scenery; take side roads to Plateau de Caussols).</td></tr>
<tr><td>Valbonne (grid-patterned old village).</td><td></td></tr>
</table>

Antibes: Château Grimaldi containing Picasso Museum, and cathedral

museum of modern Mediterranean art, including a few of the huge numbers of painters who have been profoundly influenced by the light of this coast which, little wonder, is often called the 'Mecca of modern art'.

And so to the 'Queen of the Riviera' as Nice styles itself, with some justification, even though its enormous beach is exposed and pebbly. Like Cannes and Menton, Nice used to be something of an English preserve. Until World War II, that purely English seaside phenomenon, the pier, had a representative with a casino at the end of it, suspended over the Mediterranean waters of Nice. Now, the Promenade des Anglais is the reminder of that *Belle Epoque.*

Nice is ebullient and noisy. It does not depend solely on tourism. It has a richly varied life of its own. The visitor can take part in the exhibitions, fêtes, galas, concerts. A walk along the Promenade des Anglais is entertainment enough. You pass that living Edwardian 'museum', Hôtel Negresco whose public rooms contain works of art, and its lavatories lavish ornamentation.

Red stucco arcaded buildings line one side of the harbour, Port Lympia ('port of limpid waters') from which the boats for Corsica leave. Garibaldi's birthplace in 1807 is marked by a plaque on the house at the corner of Quai Papacino.

Old Nice lies between the sea, Boulevard Jean Jaurès and the Castle (as the hill just west of the port is known; the castle was blown up in 1706; there is a lift to the top). There is plenty of

Biot where glass ornaments can be bought

sightseeing to do in the area: town hall, Baroque church of St François-de-Paul, opera house, cathedral of Ste Réparate, Chapelle de la Miséricorde of 1736 (it has an outstanding retable painted by Jean Miralhet early in the fifteenth century), a number of Genoese buildings (particularly Palais Lascaris), a remarkable Malacological Museum with exhibits of shells, Natural History Museum (Musée Barla), flower, fruit and vegetable markets in Cours Saleya (go in the mornings from Tuesday to Sunday). Food shops, bistros and an antiques market give Italian vivacity to the *Vieille Ville*.

Of all the annual festivities the Carnival, started in 1878, is the most hilarious. For a fortnight before Lent, King Carnival appears, followed by costumed processions, floats, grotesque masks, confetti showers, fireworks. King Carnival (called *Caramantran* or *Mardi Gras*) is burned in effigy on Shrove Tuesday. On Ash Wednesday is the frenetic Battle of Flowers.

Cagnes-Ville, Auguste Renoir Museum and garden with his 'Venus'

Place Masséna is the hub of the newer part of Nice. Round about is a spacious pedestrian zone with elegant shops and cafés. Further west, towards the airport,

Nice, sweep of the Promenade des Anglais

are large shopping complexes and hypermarkets.

Do not miss going to the suburb of Cimiez in the hills overlooking Nice. On the way up is the Marc Chagall Museum in Avenue Dr Ménard, specially built to

Nice: grotesque masks are a feature of annual Mardi Gras Carnival

house his seventeen canvases, 'The Biblical Message', as well as many other examples of the work of this versatile artist, who was born in 1887.

At Cimiez itself you can inspect the remains of Roman *Cemenelum* and the Archaeological Museum. Henri Matisse (1869-1954) lived in Nice for much of his later life and his art revelled in the light. He is buried close by. In the same building as the Archaeological Museum, the Matisse Museum reveals the successive influences on his work of movements in art. The church (containing three important paintings of the Nice School of 500 years ago), adjoins public gardens which look precipitously over Nice and the sea.

From Nice, long and short excursions into the dramatic scenery of its hinterland can be made. Perched villages, characteristic of Provence, are even more spectacular above the Côte d'Azur. At a distance they look grey, aloof, even distrustful; they were built for protection against incessant

Vence: outside of chapel designed and decorated by Henri Matisse

invasion. Their thick walls, narrow, steep, twisting cobbled and arcaded streets, their tiny squares and fountains, clustering towards an ancient church, are a delight to explore. Many houses are now workshops for artists and artisans where paintings, ceramics, woven cloths, jewellery or olive-wood carvings can be bought.

A few such villages within easy reach of Nice are: Tourette-sur-Loup, Gourdon, St Paul, St Jeannet (backed by a massive rock or *baou*), Gattières, Sigale, Gilette, Aspremont, Utelle, Falicon, Peillon, Peille, Coaraze.

In countless mountain village churches are the religious paintings by members of the fifteenth- and sixteenth-century School of Nice. Lucéram, as well as being a fine perched village, has a church with a number of altarpieces by Bréa and others, even though part of the Ste Marguerite retable is lodged in Musée Masséna in Nice. Lucéram had been a major centre from which the poor, itinerant artists, commissioned by Penitent Brotherhoods, and overshadowed by Italian Renaissance artists, carried their paints and brushes over mountain tracks from church to church.

THREE MOUNTAIN ITINERARIES

Nice — Grasse — Le Logis-du-Pin — St Auban — *Clue* (Gorge) de St Auban — Collongues — Clue du Riolan — Roquesteron — Clue de la Bouisse — Bouyon — Le Broc — Gattières — St Laurent-du-Var — Nice. About 200km.

Nice — N202 — follow Var valley — Défilé du Chaudan — Pont de Cians — Gorges du Cians — Beuil — Guillaumes — Gorges de Daluis — N202 — Puget-Theniers — Nice. About 200km.

Nice — D19 — Levens — valley of the Vésubie — St Jean-la-Rivière — optional drive by narrow hairpin bends to Madone d'Utelle sanctuary (1,174m), one of finest Alpes-Maritimes panoramas — Lantosque — La Bollène-Vésubie — Col de Turini — Peïra-Cava — l'Escarène — Nice. About 140km.

PLACES OF INTEREST OUTSIDE NICE

Vence: Chapelle Matisse; cathedral; Place du Peyra and fountain; old town.

St Paul: tour of ramparts; thirteenth-century church; Musée Provençal; old streets; Fondation Maeght, building, setting, modern art, special exhibitions; Colombe d'Or Hotel, restaurant and collection of modern paintings.

Villefranche: fishing port; old town; Chapelle St Pierre decorated by Jean Cocteau; St Jean-Cap Ferrat.

Beaulieu: setting; Villa Kerylos (reconstructed Greek villa).

Eze: ancient village; shops; castle ruins; Exotic Garden; views.

La Turbie: *Trophée des Alpes,* part-restored Roman monument of 6BC celebrating pacification of forty-four tribes, museum; panoramic views.

Laghet: ex-votos in sanctuary of Notre Dame and museum.

Gorges de Daluis, one of many fine mountain excursions from Nice

Before leaving Nice, a note about the origin of its name. Most books say it comes from the Greek *Nikaîa* — victory. It is more likely that the Greeks called Nice *Nikaia* — naiad, a water divinity.

East from Nice is a choice of four roads: the A8 Autoroute, and the three famous *Corniche* roads. The Grande Corniche (D2564), built by Napoleon, is the 31km high route between Nice and Menton. Use this road for the impressive views, and for visiting the majestic

Roman Trophy of the Alps at La Turbie, for the views from Hotel Vistaëro, and Roquebrune. The Moyenne Corniche (N7) also provides viewing laybys; it is the direct route to Eze. The Corniche Inférieure (N98) winds along the coast to go through Villefranche, Beaulieu, Eze-Bord-de-Mer, Cap d'Ail, Monaco, Cap Martin and Menton. Side roads connect all three *Corniches.*

Turn off at Villefranche for a drive round St Jean-Cap Ferrat for glimpses of the beautiful private estates on the peninsula. See the lighthouse, zoo, the Ile de France Museum (Fondation Ephrussi de Rothschild) with diverse treasures within and ornamental gardens. St Jean is a fishing village from which one can walk round the Pointe St Hospice, or along Promenade Maurice Rouvier; both provide lovely views of the coast to the east.

The Principality of Monaco of under 200 hectares and a population of 25,000, is a sovereign state enclave surrounded by the *département* of Alpes-Maritimes. There are no frontier formalities; only the police uniform is distinctive.

It consists of the capital town, Monaco, from whose Royal Palace the state is administered, the resort of Monte-Carlo, and the commercial centre of La Condamine. Not that much open space is available to separate one from another. So precious is land that in thirty years the Principality has transformed itself into tier on tier of skyscrapers, and reclaimed strips of land from the sea to create something by way of imported sand beaches.

Monaco's name derives from a temple to *Monoïkos* (Hercules) erected on the rock by Phoenicians. In 1308 the Grimaldis acquired Monaco from the Genoese and have ruled ever since. Their fidelity to France won them other territories along the coast. A turbulent history has seen the Principality occupied by Spaniards and French or protected by the Kingdom of Sardinia. It was incorporated with the County of Nice (roughly, the Alpes-Maritimes) into France in 1793 when the Revolutionaries renamed it *Fort Hercule.*

Independence returned at the end of the Napoleonic Wars. The rest of the Alpes-Maritimes were ceded to Italy, to return to France by the plebiscite of 1860.

Monaco was on the verge of bankruptcy and Menton and Roquebrune were sold off to France by Charles III. He struck on the lucrative idea of catering for Europe's gamblers and the casino was built on the rock named after him (Monte-Carlo). So successful was the enterprise that Monaco's wealth was drawn from it until World War II.

Today, Monaco is a highly efficient centre of business and commerce. Gambling yields only 3 per cent of revenue. The legend of glamour is still cultivated through the image of lavish, year-round programmes of entertainment, of galas, operas, Grand Prix (in May), and opulent yachts in the harbour. Such events are financed out of VAT; there is no personal taxation for Monégasques.

Still wearing its Second Empire pride, the sumptuous casino (and its gardens) sees tourists gamble in a modest way; for this you must show your passport.

Place the Oceanographic Museum high on the list of things to see in Monaco. Its aquarium, displays of marine life, and submarine exploration equipment betray the expert enthusiasm of the museum's director Jacques Cousteau.

Roquebrune, reached from the Grande Corniche, is a skilfully restored hill-village. Medieval houses, steep alleys arched over, lead up to the tenth-century castle, one of the oldest in France. It is floodlit at night. See over the furnished apartments and primitive kitchen on the third floor. Above is a terrace from which Cap Martin is seen, 300m below.

On the afternoon of August 5, you can witness scenes from the Passion enacted between the village and the chapel of La Pausa. It is a 500-year-old tradition, fulfilling a vow made in 1467 by villagers who survived the plague.

Monaco, Stade Nautique Rainier III, one of the diverse sporting attractions in the tiny Principality

A second traditional procession takes place on the evening of Good Friday, when some villagers dress as Roman soldiers, others as disciples carrying a statue of Christ. The windows of Roquebrune are decorated with flowers and upturned empty snail shells holding lighted wicks. The procession is known in Provençal as *Proucessioun dei Limassa,* the Procession of the Snails. Its

EXCURSION TO VAL DES MERVEILLES

Beautiful, inhospitable mountain and lake scenery round Mont Bégo (2,873m) in Parc National du Mercantour. Four valleys with some 46,000 prehistoric rock-carvings by Ligurian tribes. Earliest 7,000 years ago. Geometric carvings: human figures, spears, hatchets, axes, daggers, agricultural tools, bovine heads, horns, half-moons. Visits Jun-Oct only.

Route: Menton — D2566 — Sospel (medieval bridge) — D2204 — Col de Brouis (879m) — N204 — Gorges de Saorge — Gorges de Bergue — left before St Dalmas — Les Mesches — Casterino (73km).

Inns at Casterino: Auberge des Melèzes (9 rooms).
Tel: (93) 04 64 95
Auberge Marie Madeleine (11 rooms).
Tel: (93) 04 65 93
Val Casterino (12 rooms).
Tel: (93) 04 64 38

Jeep and guide hired through hotel; make up party to reduce cost. Dress for high-altitude walks. Marked paths for experienced walkers. Refuge Les Merveilles hut of Club Alpin Français on GR5.

Initial enquiries at Office de Tourisme, Palais de l'Europe, Avenue Boyer, Menton.
Tel: (93) 57 57 00

religious name is Procession of the Entombment of Christ. Some say the ritual dates back to 1316, the snails being the Christian symbol of resurrection.

On the Menton road, 200m beyond Roquebrune is an olive tree, thought to be 1,000 years old.

Although much added to with modern buildings outside the old town, Menton

*Sospel, reached by one of
the beguiling valleys
leading out of Menton*

Monaco, the Exotic Gardens

La Napoule

Monte Carlo Harbour

Royal Palace, Monte Carlo

remains a picture postcard Italianate town. Tall, honey-coloured houses rise gracefully from near the sea to the church of St Michel. Outside the church the prestigious chamber-music festival is held under floodlights during the first half of August.

Menton's setting is idyllic. The mountains stand well back, respectfully, yet giving the town its enviable winter climate which allows lemon crops to ripen; the lemon festival is held in February.

Compared with other resorts along the coast, Menton retains a more leisurely atmosphere. Clamber about the old town, particularly Rue Longue; stroll along the Promenade du Soleil past the casino to the harbour and the Cocteau Museum there; along Boulevard du Garavan. The cemetery is interesting for the well-known English names, for Menton was first a health resort for the treatment of tuberculosis on the initiative of the English specialist, Dr Henry Bennet, in the 1860s.

Beyond the encircling arches of the Autoroute and into the hills are the attractive villages of Ste Agnès, Gorbio, Monti, Castillon, Castellar and Peille; five roads along five valleys lead inland from Menton.

Foundation Maeght at St Paul-de-Vence, a showcase of modern art

Further Information

Every resort and large town, as well as many of the smaller towns, has a tourist information centre called *Office de Tourisme* or *Syndicat d'Initiative*. Information about hotels, camp sites, excursions, museums, special events, etc can be obtained there. In larger resorts emergency-only hotel accommodation can be arranged.

Addresses and telephone numbers (and when open) of these offices are given below town-entries in the annual *Guide Michelin*.

TELEPHONE CALLS

Public telephones are to be found in post offices (PTT), some cafés and in street kiosks in towns and villages. Coins of 50 centimes, 1 and 5 franc pieces are inserted.

Telephone numbers consist of six figures plus a two-figure prefix (shown in brackets) which stands for the district (usually equivalent to the *département*). This prefix is not dialled for calls within that district. To make a call from outside the district the numbers 16 must be dialled first, then the prefix numbers, then the six-figure number.

A shrill intermittent tone indicates that the number is ringing; a more rapid and softer tone is the engaged signal.

OUTDOOR CENTRES OF INTEREST AND ENTERTAINMENT

Aigues-Mortes
Salins du Midi (south of town).
Guided visits to saltings, Tue-Fri pm, July and Aug. Enquire at Tourist Office, Place St Louis.
Tel: (66) 51 95 00.

La Barben
Château de la Barben (8km east of Salon).
Aquarium, vivarium, miniature railway, zoo.
Open: 10am to dusk. Apartment rooms open 10am-12 noon, 2-6pm. Closed Tuesday.

Le Beausset
Circuit Automobile Paul Ricard (8km north off N8).
Frequent motor-racing events, karting, vintage racing-car museum. Details from Circuit Paul Ricard, 83330 Le Beausset.
Tel: (94) 93 55 19.

La Brague
Marineland (off N7 on Biot road).
Marine, zoo, dolphins, aquaria, children's play area.
Open: daily 10am-6pm.
Tel: (93) 34 49 51.

Cagnes-sur-Mer
Hippodrome de la Côte d'Azur racecourse, on N98.
Varied programmes include trotting under lights. Season Dec-Mar, Aug-Sep. See local newspapers.

Camargue
Réserve Zoologique et Botanique.
Accredited naturalists and students
only. Apply in advance to Réserve
Nationale, La Capelière, 13200 Arles.

Cap d'Antibes
Jardin Thuret, Boulevard J.F. Kennedy.
Rare and exotic trees and plants;
important agronomic research centre.
Closed Sat and Sun.

Château Gombert
Baumo Loubière (2km north-west).
Caves, polychrome stalactites and
stalagmites.
Open: pm daily except Tue; am Sun and
public holidays.

Cuges-les-Pins
OK Corral. Amusement park.
Open: daily 10am-6.30pm, April-Sept;
Wed, Sat, Sun in Mar and Oct. Closed
Nov-Feb.

Entraigues
Mr Joël Moyne, Domaine St Sauveur.
Hire of horse-drawn gipsy caravans and
instruction.
Tel: (90) 83 16 26.

Entraigues
Ranch de l'Etalon Blanc.
Hire of riding horses.
Tel: (90) 83 17 68.

Eze
Jardin Exotique, below ruined castle.
Cacti.
Open daily until dusk.

Fos
Port complex. Guided boat tours. Apply
in advance to Service des Relations
Publiques du Port Autonome de
Marseille, 23 Place de la Joliette, 13000
Marseille.

Fréjus
Parc Zoologique (5km north, right off
D4 Bagnols road over autoroute).
Animals and birds in natural
environment. Open all year.
Tel: (94) 40 70 65.

Fréjus
Safari de l'Esterel (near Parc
Zoologique).
Birds; wild animals viewed from closed
car windows. Closed Tue, Nov-Easter.
Tel: (94) 40 70 60.

Gémenos
Parc St Pons (3km west, off D2).
Water-mill, spring, ruins, unusual trees.
Closed Tues.

Hyères
Jardins Olbius Riquier, Avenue Olbius
Riquier.
Tel: (94) 57 77 19.

Marseille
Jardin Zoologique (behind Palais
Longchamp).
Wild animals. Open all year.

Marseille
Le Port. Entry by Gate 2 on foot.
Open: Sun and public holidays.
Tel: (91) 91 90 66.

Méjanes
Paul Ricard ranch in Camargue near
north shore of Etang de Vacarrès.
Holiday centre, scenic railway, horse-
riding and shows, branding of bulls,
mock bull-fights.

Menton
Jardin des Colombières, Boulevard de
Garavan.
Mediterranean garden.
Open: am and pm daily.

Menton
Jardin Botanique Exotique Villa Val
Rahmeh, Chemin de St Jacques.
State owned, Mediterranean and
tropical flora.
Closed Tues.
Tel: (93) 35 86 72.

Monaco
Centre d'Acclimatation Zoologique,
Place du Canton.
Anthropoid apes.
Open all year.
Tel: (93) 30 18 31.

Monaco
Jardin Exotique, Boulevard du Jardin
Exotique.
Cacti. Grotte de l'Observatoire,
stalactites and stalagmites.
Open all year.
Tel: (93) 30 33 65 and 30 33 66.

Pont de Gau
Camargue bird sanctuary. Daily.

Port Cros
National Park Nature Reserve.
Boat services from Le Lavandou in 35
mins; also from Toulon, La Tour
Fondue, Hyères-Plage, Cavalaire.
Guided botanical rambles and
underwater diving, June-Sept.
Information from 50 Avenue Gambetta,
83400 Hyères.
Tel: (94) 63 32 98.

St Cézaire
Grottes de St Cézaire (3km north-east
on D613).
Guided tours of coloured concretions.
Daily 10am-12 noon, 2-6pm. Closed
Nov-Feb.

St Jean-Cap Ferrat
Jardin Zoologique, Vivarium du Cap
Ferrat, Boulevard Général de Gaulle.
Animals, reptiles, birds. Daily.
Tel: (93) 01 31 56.

St Martin-Vésubie
Réserve de Chasse du Mercantour.
(Approch from Le Boréon, 8km north-
east by D89).
Wildlife reserve and summer
mountaineering centre. Information
from Tourist Office, St Martin-Vésubie,
Place Félix Faure, or Rue Maccarani,
06000 Nice.
Tel: (93) 87 86 10.

Sanary
Jardin Exotique et Zoologique Sanary-
Bandol (6km towards Bandol on N559,
right on D559a and right again).
Tropical plants and animals, rock
garden, greenhouses. Open all year.
Tel: (94) 29 40 36.

La Seyne-sur-Mer
Jardin Animalier, Forêt de Janas.
Small zoo. Closed Tue.

Le Thor
Grotte de Thouzon (2km north on D16).
Stalactites. Closed Jan and Feb except
Sun.

Toulon
Jardin Zoologique, Super-Toulon.
Open all day all year.

Toulon
Aerial cableway from Super-Toulon to
Mont Faron (542m).
10 min service am and pm all year for
views.

Five waymarked footpaths of varying difficulty cover some of the region's most striking scenery. They are part of a network covering the whole country, and their Provençal sections are marked on Michelin maps 81 and 84 (1:200,000) by broken lines with their identification numbers (GR4, GR5 etc). Detailed illustrated guides known as *Topo-guides* can be bought at local bookshops. Fuller information can be obtained from the responsible organisation, Comité National des Sentiers de Grande Randonnée (CNSGR), 92 rue de Clignancourt, 75018 Paris. Tel: 259 60 40.

In Provence, the main places the footpaths make for are:

GR4 Méditerranée — Océan
Vaison-la-Romaine — Malaucène — Sault — Simiane-la-Rotonde — Oppedette — Céreste — Manosque — Gréoux-les-Bains — Riez — Moustiers — Gorges du Verdon by the Sentier Martel — Castellane — Entrevaux — St Cassien — Gréolières — Cipières — St Lambert — Grasse.

GR5 Hollande — Méditerranée
Larche — St Etienne-de-Tinée — Auron — Roya — St Sauveur-sur-Tinée — Rimplas — St Dalmas-Valdeblore — Utelle — Aspremont — Nice.

GR52 St Dalmas-Valdeblore— Boréon — La Madone de Fenestre — Pas du Mont Colomb — Refuge Nice — Refuge des Merveilles — Sospel — Menton.

GR9 Jura — Côte-d'Azur
Brantes — Mont Ventoux — Sault - St Saturnin-d'Apt — Buoux — Vaugines — Cucuron — Beaumont-de-Pertuis — Trets — Hôtellerie de la Ste Baume — Signes — Belgentier — Pignans — La Garde-Freinet — St Paul-les-Mûres.

GR6 Alpes — Océan
St Paul-sur-Ubaye — Barcelonnette — Seynes-les-Alpes — Sisteron — Forcalquier — Vachères — Oppedette — Viens — Rustrel — Roussillon — Eygalières — Les Baux — Tarascon.

ANNUAL EVENTS

Aix-en-Provence
Mid-July to mid-Aug, music festival.

Allauch
Sun following 24 June, Festival of St John, blessing of animals.
24 Dec, Provençal midnight mass.

Antibes
Sun after 29 June, Festival of St Peter, procession to harbour.

Apt
Whit Sun and Mon, cavalcade, music festival.
Last week in July, pilgrimage of Ste Anne.

Arles
Easter Fri to Mon, bullfight festival.
Last Sun in April, *Fête des Gardians*.
July, international festival of music, dance, drama in Roman theatre.
July, international photography festival.
Mid-Dec to mid-Jan, *Santons* trade fair.

Avignon
Last 3 weeks of July, international drama festival, mainly in Great Courtyard of Palais de Papes.
14 July, firework display.
15 July, jousting on Rhône.

Barjols
16 Jan every 4 years, *Fête du St Marcel.*

Les Baux
24 Dec, midnight mass in St Vincent church and pageant of Nativity.

Beaucaire
End July to early Aug, Fête to commemorate medieval fair.

Le Beausset
Early April, 'Moto Journal 200' motor race.
Mid-Sept, *Bol d' Or* motor race.

Bollène
Last Sat in June, *Fête du Papagaî.*

Boulbon
1 June, Bottle Procession of St Marcellin, and blessing of wine.

Cairanne
July, wine festival.

Cannes
Feb, mimosa festival.
Mar, photography and amateur cinema festival.
May, international film festival.
July-Aug, *Nuits des Leirins.*
Aug, fireworks festival.
Sept, international yachting festival; royal regatta.
Sept, festival of vintage cars.
Oct-Nov, international golf championships.

Carpentras
July, festival of Notre-Dame de Santé.

Cavaillon
1st Mon in Sept, traditional festival.

Châteauneuf-du-Pape
24 and 25 April, festival of St Marc.
1 May, lily of the valley festival.

Courthézon
End June, vine-stock festival.

Cucuron
Sat after 21 May, procession with poplar tree in honour of Ste Tulle.

Digne
First Sun in Aug, lavender festival.

Entrevaux
Weekend nearest 24 Jan, Fête of St John the Baptist.
2 weeks in Aug, sixteenth- and seventeenth-century music festival.

Fontaine-de-Vaucluse
Mid-June to mid-Sept, *son-et-lumière.*
July, *Festival de la Sorgue.*

Fréjus
3rd Sun after Easter, *Bravade* costume procession.

Grasse
Last 2 weeks July, international amateur music, folk and drama festival.

Graveson
Last Sun in July, festival of St Eloi.

Ile Ste Marguerite
1 June to 15 Sept, *son-et-lumière* at fort.

L'Isle-sur-la-Sorgue
Mar, international moto-cross.

Istres
1st Sun in Aug, *Fête de St Pierre,*
jousting, bullfighting.

Lagarde-Paréol
May, international moto-cross.

Lagnes
Mardi Gras, *Fête du Caramentran.*

Marseille
2 weeks from 1st Sun in Nov, *Santons*
fair on La Canebière.

Martigues
1st Sat in July, nocturnal cavalcade of
jousting boats.

Menton
Week before Shrove Tuesday, lemon
festival. 1st half of Aug, international
festival of chamber music in floodlit
Place de l'Eglise.

Monaco
27 Jan, Monte-Carlo motor rally.
27 Jan, festival of Ste Dévote.
Feb, international television festival.
April, international tennis
championships.
May, Monaco Grand Prix.
July to Aug, international fireworks
festival.
Aug to Sept, world amateur theatre
festival.
Nov, Monégasque National Fête.
Dec, international circus festival.

Mondragon
May, *Fête du Drac.*

Monteux
Sun after 15 May, festival of St Gens.
Tue after last Sun in Aug, fireworks
display.

Nice
2 weeks before Lent, Carnival, firework
display (Shrove Tue), Battle of Flowers
(day after Ash Wed).
April, international dog show.
Each Sun in May, *Fête des Maïs* in
Cimiez Gardens.
May, spring music festival.
July, grand jazz parade in Cimiez
Gardens.
July, international folklore festival.
Aug, wine festival in Cimiez Gardens.
Oct, autumn music festival.

Orange
Last 2 weeks in July, international music
festival in Roman theatre.

Pernes-les-Fontaines
May, international moto-cross.

Piolenc
End Aug, garlic festival.

Roquebrune-Cap Martin
Good Friday evening, procession of the
Entombment of Christ.
5 Aug, afternoon, procession of the
Passion.

St Paul-de-Vence
2nd fortnight in July, *Nuits de la
Fondation Maeght.*

St Tropez
16-18 May, *Bravade de St Torpes.*
15 June, *Fête des Espagnols,* the Spanish
bravade.
Once a month in July and Aug, classical
concerts in Citadel.

La Ste Baume
21-22 July, festival of Mary Magdalene
and midnight mass.

Ste Cécile-les-Vignes
1 May, moto-cross.

Les Ste Maries-de-la-Mer
24-25 May, *Pèlerinage des Gitanes,*
Gipsy celebrations.
Sun nearest 24 July, *Fête Virginenco.*
Weekend nearest 22 Oct, gipsy
pilgrimage.
1st Sun in Dec, gipsy pilgrimage.

Séguret
Apr to Sept, ethnological exhibition.
2nd fortnight in Aug, Provençal festival.
July to Aug, and Dec-Jan, exhibition of
santons (clay figurines).
3rd Sun in Aug, *bravade.*
24 Dec, mystery play.

Signes
Sun nearest 24 June, festival of St Eloi.

Sisteron
Mid-July and mid-Aug, festival of
drama, music and dance.

Tarascon
Last Sun in June, *Fête de la Tarasque.*

Toulon
April, flower festival.
July to Aug, festival of circus artistes.
Nov, *santons* fair.

Vaison-la-Romaine
Early July, international folklore
festival.
Mid-July to mid-Aug, theatre and music
festival in Roman Theatre.
1st Sun after 15 Aug, Provençal festival.
24 Dec, midnight mass and Provençal
mystery play.

Valréas
23 Jun at 10.15pm, noctural procession
of 'Petit St Jean' (500 years old).
July and Aug, musical evenings, theatre.
1st Sun and Mon in Aug, lavender fair.
Christmas to Jan, *santons* cribs.

Vence
Easter Sun and Mon, Battle of Flowers.
Provençal dancing.

Ventabren
24 Dec, Nativity play.

Villeneuve-lès-Avignon
End April, festival of St Marc.
July, international summer festival of
music, dancing, theatre, poetry, art and
cultural exhibitions, workshops.

MUSEUMS, ART GALLERIES AND
BUILDINGS OPEN TO THE PUBLIC

Most State-run museums and art
galleries are open from 9.00, 9.30 or
10.00am until noon, and from 2.00pm to
7.00pm in summer and 6.00pm in
winter. They are closed on Tuesdays.
Where times of opening differ markedly
from those above, an indication is given
in the list which follows.
   It is well to check that a place is open
on French Public Holidays. These are: 1
January (New Year's Day); Easter
Sunday and Monday; 1 May (Labour
Day), 8 May (VE Day); Ascension Day;
Whit Sunday and Monday; 14 July
(Bastille Day); 15 August (Assumption
Day); 1 November (All Saints' Day); 11
November (Armistice Day); 25
December (Christmas Day).
   Many rural churches and chapels
contain things of interest, but are
opened only on demand. They are not
included here. Keen students of church
art can enquire locally where the key
may be obtained.

Aigues-Mortes
Tour de Constance and Ramparts.
Guided tours available.

Aix-en-Provence
Atelier Cézanne.
9 Avenue Paul Cézanne.
Tel: (42) 21 06 53.

Musée Granet (Musée des Beaux-Arts),
Place St Jean.
Tel: (42) 38 14 70.

Musée Paul Arbaud,
2a Rue du 4-Septembre.
Open: 2-5pm summer only and closed
Wed.

Musée des Tapisseries,
Ancien Archevêché, Place des Martyres
de la Résistance.
Guided tours available.
Tel: (42) 23 09 91.

Fondation Vasarely,
Avenue Marcel Pagnol. (4km west-
south-west).
Tel: (42) 20 01 09.

Pavillon de Vendôme,
34 Rue Célony.
Tel: (42) 21 05 78.

Muséum d'Histoire Naturelle,
Hôtel Boyer d'Eguilles, 6 Rue Espariat.
Closed Sun am.

Bibliothèque Méjanes,
Hôtel de Ville, Place de l'Hôtel-de-Ville.
Fondation St John Perse in one wing.
Open to scholars who apply in advance
to curator.

Musée du Vieil Aix,
17 Rue Gaston de Saporta.
Closed Mon and Feb.

Plateau d'Entremont
(2½km north). Celto-Ligurian
excavations.

Allauch
Musée du Vieux Allauch,
Place Pierre Bellot.
Open: Wed and Sat 3-6pm; Sun and
public holidays 10am-12 noon, 3-6pm.

Ansouis
Château de Sabran.
Open: daily 2.30-6.30pm; closed Tues
Oct-June.

Musée Extraordinaire.
Open: 2-7pm daily, except Tues.

Antibes
Musée Archéologique,
Bastion St André.
Closed Nov.

Musée Picasso,
Château Grimaldi, Vieille Ville.
Tel: (93) 33 67 67.
Guided tours available. Closed Nov.

Apt
Musée Archéologique,
Place Carnot.
Closed Tues and Sun.

Arles
Single ticket gives entry to museums
marked *.

*Les Alyscamps,
Rue Pierre Renaudel.

*Arènes,
Rond Point des Arènes.

**Musèe d'Art Chrétien and
Cryptoporticus,*
Rue Balze.

*Musée d'Art Païen,
Rue de la République.

*Musée Réattu,
Rue du Grand Prieuré.

*Théâtre Antique,
Rue du Cloître.

*Palais Constantin,
Thermes de la Trouille, Rue D. Maïsto.
When doorkeeper not available, apply
Musée Réattu.

St Trophime,
Rue de l'Hôtel-de-Ville, and Cloître St
Trophime, Place de la République.
Open daily.

Muséon Arlaten,
Rue de la République.
Closed Mon.

Les Arcs-sur-Argens
Château de Ste Rosseline.
Chapel only. Daily 2-6pm.

Aubagne
Musée de la Légion Etrangère, Camp de
la Demande.
Open: daily June-Sept; Wed, Sat, Sun
Oct-May.

Aulan
Château.
Open summer only.

Avignon
Palais des Papes,
Place du Palais.
Includes museum of medieval painting
and sculpture. Hourly or half-hourly
guided tours daily throughout year.
Multi-language guided tours available.
Musée Calvet and Musée Esprit Requien,
Rue Joseph Vernet.
Requien library and herbarium for
specialists only.
Tel: (90) 86 33 84.

Musée Lapidaire,
27 Rue de la République.

Musée du Petit Palais,
Place du Palais.
Tel: (90) 86 44 58.

Palais du Roure,
Hôtel de Baroncelli-Javon, Rue du
Collège-du-Roure.
Museum open daily. Fondation
Flandreysy-Esperandicu, for study of
Provençal and Mediterranean
civilisation (available to sponsored
artists and writers).

Pont St Bénézet and Chapelle St Nicolas.
Apply to bridgekeeper on quay.
Closed 15-31 Jan, 15 Feb-3 Mar, Fri
Nov-Mar.

Musée Aubanel,
(south of Palais des Papes).
Open: 9-11am. Closed Sat, Sun and
Aug.

Fondation Jean Vilar,
Hôtel de Crochans, Rue de Mons.
History of post-war French theatre.

Musée Vouland,
17 Rue Victor Hugo.
Seventeenth- and eighteenth-century
decorative arts. Tues-Fri, am and pm, 1
July-30 Sept; Tues-Fri, pm only 30 Sept-
1 July (on Tues group visits only).

Barbentane
Château.
Open: daily, mid-Mar to Nov; closed
Wed, Mar-May and Oct; open Sun only
Nov to mid-Mar.

Le Barroux
Château.
Accompanied visits to chapel, July and
Aug.

Les Baux
Musée d'Art Moderne,
Hôtel Manville.
Mid-Mar to Oct, am and pm.

Musée Lapidaire,
Hôtel de la Tour-de-Brau.
Ticket includes access to deserted
village.

Musée Archéologique,
Hôtel des Porcelets.

Ile de Bendor
Musée Mondial des Vins et des Spiritueux
(By boat from Bandol in 5 mins).
Closed Wed.

Beaucaire
Château.
Guided tours only.
Closed Fri.

Musée du Vieux Beaucaire,
27 Rue Barbès.
Limited and variable opening.

Musée Lapidaire,
Rue de Nîmes.

Beaulieu-sur-Mer
Villa Kerylos.
Guided tours only.
Open pm all year. Closed Mon and Nov.

Biot
Musée Fernand Leger.

Bollène
Musée Municipal.

Musée Pasteur,
Quartier du Puy.
Regional paintings, ancient coins.
Closed Tues.

Bonnieux
Musée de la Boulangerie,
Rue de la République.

Bonpas
Chartreuse de Bonpas.
Gardens only.
Visits to fourteenth-century
charterhouse by authorisation.

Bormes-les-Mimosas
Hôtel de Ville.
Works of art.
Closed Sun and public holidays.

Brignoles
Musée du Pays Brignolais.
Closed Tues and Sept.

Abbaye de la Celle (3km south).
By permission of hotel director, visit old
conventual buildings, Mar-Dec.

Le Brusc — Ile des Embiez
Fondation Océanographique Ricard
(Boat from Le Brusc in 10 mins).
Permission to visit museum and
aquarium from Fondation, Ile des
Embiez, 83140 Le Brusc.
Tel: (94) 25 01 31.

Buoux
Fort.
Open daily all year.

Cagnes
Château-Musée,
Haut-de-Cagnes.
Includes Musée d'Art Moderne
Méditerranéen and Musée de l'Olivier.
Closed Tues and mid-Oct to mid-Nov.

Notre Dame de Protection,
Haute-de-Cagnes.
Open pm, closed Tues and mid-Oct to
mid-Nov.

Musée Renoir,
Avenue des Collettes.
Tel: (93) 20 61 07.
Open pm, closed Tues and mid-Oct to
mid-Nov.

Camargue
Musée Boumian (1km north of Stes
Maries on N570).
Museum of Camargue life.

Centre d'Information
Ginès, 5km north of Stes Maries.
Tel: (90) 97 86 32.
Camargue information centre.
Closed Sat and Sun in winter.

Musée Camarguais,
Pont de Rousty (10km south-west of
Arles; left off N570).
Closed Tues Sept-April.

Cannes
Tour du Suquet
(Tour du Mont Chevalier).
Apply to custodian.

Musée Jean-Gabriel Domergue,
Villa Fiesole, Avenue Fiesole.
Open: daily 3-7pm, April-Sept; Closed
Sun and public holidays.

Musée La Castre,
Le Suquet.
Tel: (93) 39 98 98.
Closed Mon and Nov.

Observatoire de Super-Cannes,
3km north of Cannes.
Open: daily; Sat and Sun only in Nov.

Ile Ste Marguerite
(15 min by boat from Cannes, Gare
Maritime).
Fort Royal *Son-et-lumière* certain
evenings in summer.
Closed mid-July to mid-Aug.

Ile St Honorat
(30 min by boat from Cannes, Gare
Maritime).
Château.
Open: daily June-Sept.

Ile St Honorat,
Monastery and Musée Lapidaire.

Cap d'Antibes
Sanctuaire de la Garoupe.
Open daily all year.

Musée Naval et Napoléonien,
Batterie du Grillon, Avenue Kennedy.
Tel: (93) 61 45 32.
Open: am and pm all year.

Le Phare,
Lighthouse open daily to one hour
before sunset.

Carpentras
Synagogue,
Rue d'Inguimbert.
Closed Sat.

Musée Duplessis,
Hôtel d'Allemand,
Boulevard Albin Durand.
Closed Wed.

*Musée des Beaux-Arts et Musée
Comtadin,*
(as above.)
Closed Wed.
Also Bibliothèque Inguimbertine. Visits
by appointment.
Closed Sat pm, Sun, Mon am.

Hôtel-Dieu,
Avenue Victor Hugo.
Closed Sat and Sun.

Musée Sobirats
(Musée d'Art Decoratif),
11 Rue du Collège.
Apply to porter.

Musée Archéologique,
Rue des Stes-Maries.
Apply to caretaker at Musée des Beaux-
Arts.

Musée de la Poésie,
Route de Pernes-les-Fontaines.
Tel: (90) 63 19 49.
Open: daily 2-5pm.

Cassis
Musée de Peinture,
Hôtel de Ville.
Open: 9.30-11.30am Wed and Fri.

Cavaillon
Musée Archéologique,
Grande Rue.

Synagogue & Musée Judéo-Comtadin,
6 Rue Chabran.

Chapelle St Jacques,
(5½km west on D938 by car; 15 min on foot up steps).
Open: daily 1.30-6.30pm.

Château-Gombert
Musée d'Art Local.
Open: Mon, Sat, Sun pm.

Châteauneuf-du-Pape
Les Caves du Père Anselme.
Exhibition of old presses and tools.
Open: daily.

Châteauneuf-lès-Martigues
Musée du Castrum Vetus,
4 Montée des Ruines.
Tel: (91) 88 84 83.
Open: Sun and public holidays 3.30-6.30pm.

La Ciotat
Musée d'Histoire Locale,
Rue des Poilus.
Open: 5-7pm Sat, Sun 10am-12 noon, Wed 2.30-5.30pm.

Cogolin
Les Tapis et Tissues de Cogolin,
Boulevard Louis Blanc.
Open: Mon-Fri, guided tours.

La Maison du Liège
(on N98 towards St Tropez).
Cork-oak workshop.

Courrieu,
58 Avenue Clémenceau.
Briar-pipe workshop.

Collobrières
Chartreuse de la Verne (12km east).
Closed Tues, Oct-Jun.

Colmars
Fort de Savoie.
Open: July and Aug.

Cucuron
Musée du Luberon
(Musée Marc Deydier),
Hôtel des Bouliers.
Closed Thur.

Digne
Musée Municipal,
Boulevard de Gassendi.
Closed Mon and am Sun.

Draguignan
Musée-Bibliothèque,
Rue de la République.
Closed Sun, Mon and Aug.

Tour d'Horloge,
Montée de l'Horloge.
Keys at Tourist Office, 9 Boulevard Clémenceau.
Tel: (94) 68 05 05.

Entrecasteaux
Château-Musée.
Tel: (94) 04 43 95.
Open daily all year.

Entrevaux
Musée Historial.
Waxworks, arms and armour.

Eze
Musée d'Histoire Locale.

Fontanine-de-Vaucluse
Musée Norbert Casteret,
Chemin de la Fontaine.
Speleological exhibition.
Open: am and pm in summer; apply to museum out of season.

Musée Pétrarque.
Open: daily.

Vallis Clausa paper-mill,
Handmade paper as in fourteenth
century.

Cristallerie des Papes,
Demonstrations of glass-blowing.

Musée des Restrictions.
Exhibition of rationing and war-time
restrictions (1940-5).
Open: 1-6.30pm daily, except Mon.

Fontvieille
Moulin de Daudet (south on D33).
Open: daily.
Guided tours available.

Forcalquier
*Musée Archéologique et d'Histoire
Locale,*
Place du Bourguet.
Open: May-Sept 10-11am, 4-5pm; rest of
year 3-5pm. Closed Mon am, Wed, Sat
pm, Sun and public holidays.

Couvent des Cordeliers.
Open: am and pm Apr-Sept; pm only for
rest of year.

Fos-sur-Mer
Musée Archéologique,
Ancienne Petite Chapelle Notre Dame-
de-la-Mer.
Tel: (42) 05 01 22.
Open: Sat and Sun 3-6.45pm.

La Fossette
Centre de Vie (8km north-west on
N568).
Fos Complex Community Information
Centre: exhibition, films, models of
industrial complex, arboretum.
Open all year.

Fréjus
Cité Episcopal,
Place de Formigé.
Guided tours of cloister, baptistry,
museum.

Les Arènes (Roman amphitheatre).
Closed Tues and Oct. Bullfights in July
and Aug.

Pagode Boudhique (2km on N7 towards
Cannes, off right).
July-Aug 3-6.30pm; Sept-June 3-5pm on
Wed, Sat, Sun.

Ganagobie
Prieuré.
Guided tours daily.

Gordes
Château & Musée Vasarely.
Tel: (90) 72 02 89.
Open am and pm all year.

Musée du Vitrail, Moulin des Bouillons
(4½km south on D148).
Open all year.

Musée Paléontologique Insula-Maria.

Village des Bories
(3km south-west; right on rough track
beyond join of D15 and D2).
Open: 9am-sunset, Feb to mid-Nov;
10am-sunset, Sat and Sun, mid-Nov to
Jan.

Gourdon
Château.
Open: 11am-1pm Jun-Sept; 2-6pm Oct-
May. Closed Tues.

Grasse
Maison Fragonard,
Boulevard Fragonard.
Guided tours of factory, am and pm all
year.
Museum open am and pm all year.
Closed Sun.

Villa-Musée Fragonard,
Boulevard Fragonard.
Closed Mon and Nov, also 2nd and 3rd
Sun of each month.

Musée Amiral de Grasse,
Hôtel de Pontèves, Boulevard du Jeu-
de-Ballon.
Closed Mon and Nov, also 2nd and 3rd
Sun of each month.

Musée d'Art et Histoire de Provence,
Rue Mirabeau.
Closed Mon and Nov, also 2nd and 3rd
Sun of each month.

Hospice Petit-Paris,
Boulevard Victor Hugo.
Paintings in chapel. Apply caretaker.

Grignan
Château.
Closed Tues and 1 May.

Musée Faure-Cabrol.
Open: am and pm.

Hyères
Musée Municipal,
Place Lefevre.
Open: am and pm weekdays except
Tues; Sat and Sun pm only.

L'Isle-sur-la-Sorgue
Musée Bibliothèque René Char,
20 Rue du Dr Tallet.
Relates to distinguished native of town,
present-day poet.

Hôtel-Dieu.
Open: am and pm.
Apply to caretaker.

Istres
Musée du Vieil Istres.
Open: May-Sept. Closed Tues.

Laghet
Musée Notre Dame de Laghet.
Contains, with Sanctuary of Notre
Dame de Laghet next door, collections
of ex-votos.

Lambesc
Musée du Vieux Lambesc,
Route de Salon.
Tel: (42) 28 01 64 or (42) 24 03 83.
Folklore and crafts.

Lavéra
Oil refineries of Société Français des
Pétroles BP.
Apply to Service d'Information SFBP,
Poste Restante 1, 13117 Lavéra.

Les Lecques — La Madrague
Musée de Tauroentum.
Open: 3-7pm June-Sept; 2-5pm Sat and
Sun Oct-May.

Lourmarin
Château
(Académie d'Aix-en-Provence).
Open: 9-11.45am, 2.30-5.45pm June-
Sept; 2-4.45pm Oct-May. Closed Tues,
Oct-Easter.

Maillane
Muséon Mistral.

Mane
Château de Sauvan (2km south on
N100).
Open: 3-7pm Wed, Thur, Sat, Sun and
public holidays.

Marcoule
Centre Atomique de Marcoule.
Museum and viewing platform.
Open: daily all year.

Marignane
Château des Mirabeau,
Hôtel de Ville.
Rooms of the Marquis open during
office hours.

Marseille
Musée des Vestiges,
Rue Henri Barbusse.
Greek remains.
Open: daily all year.

Musée du Vieux Marseille,
Rue de la Prison.
Closed Tues and am Wed.

Ancienne Cathédrale de la Major.
Closed Fri. Guided tours only.

Musée de la Marine,
In Bourse.
Open: daily all year.

Musée Cantini,
Rue Grignan.
Closed Tues and am Wed.

Château Borély,
Avenue Clot-Bey.
Contains Musée d'Archéologie
Méditerranéenne, Musée Lapidaire and
Jardin Botanique.
Museums open 9.30am-12.15pm,
1-5pm; closed Tues and am Wed.
Botanic garden open 9am-5pm; closed
weekends.
Tel: (91) 73 21 60.

Musée des Docks Romains,
28 Place Vivaux.
Tel: (91) 91 24 62.
Closed Tues and am Wed.

Musée Grobet-Labadié,
140 Boulevard Longchamp.
Tel: (91) 62 21 82.
Closed Tues and am Wed.

Musée des Beaux-Arts,
Palais Longchamp, Boulevard
Longchamp.
Closed Tues and am Wed.

Muséum d'Histoire Naturelle,
Palais Longchamp.
Closed Tues and am Wed.

Basilique St Victor,
Rue Sainte.
Crypt open am and pm Mon-Sat and pm
Sun.

Château d'If,
(daily boat services from Quai des
Belges, Old Port).
Medieval castle on islet.

Marsillargues
Château de Teillan
Open: 2-6pm June-Sept. Closed Mon.

Martigues
Musée du Vieux-Martigues.
Open: 2-5pm all year. Closed Tues.

Musée des Beaux-Arts,
Quartier Ferrières (in old Custom
House).
Open: 2-7pm all year. Closed Tues.

Mazan
Musée Communal,
Rue St Lazaire.
Open: pm daily, July and Aug; pm June,
Sept, Sun and public holidays.

Menton
Musée Cocteau,
Quai Napoléon.
Closed Mon, Tues and Nov.

Salle des Mariages,
Hôtel de Ville, Rue de la République.
Guided tours of Jean Cocteau's murals
available.
Open: am and pm all year. Closed Tues
and Nov.

Musée Municipal,
Rue Lorédan-Larchey.
Open: am and pm all year. Closed Tues
and Nov.

Musée Carnolès,
3 Avenue de la Madone.
Tel: (93) 35 49 71.
Antique and modern paintings.
Closed Mon and Tues.

Monaco
Musée d'Anthropologie Préhistorique,
Boulevard du Jardin Exotique.
Tel: (93) 30 33 65 and 30 33 66.
Open: daily 9am-sunset.

Musée National (Collection Galéa),
Avenue Princesse-Grace.
Guided tours available.
Open: am and pm daily.

Musée Océanographique,
Avenue St Martin.
Tel: (93) 30 15 14.
Open: 9am-10.30pm July-Aug; 9am or
9.30am-7pm rest of year.

Palais du Prince,
Place du Palais.
Includes Musée Napoléon.
Palace open am and pm July-Sept.
Guided tours only. Museum closed
Mon.

Montmajour
Abbaye de Montmajour.
Closed Tues and Wed.

Moustiers-Ste-Marie
Musée des Faïences.
Open: am and pm all year.

La Napoule
Château de la Napoule,
Fondation Henry Clews.
Open: daily except Tues 3-5pm. Closed
three weeks in Dec. Guided tours only.

Nice
All museums marked * are run by the
Municipality and are free.

* *Musée Masséna,*
65 Rue de France.
Tel: (93) 88 11 34.
Closed Mon and some public holidays.

* *Musée Jules Chéret* (Musée des Beaux-
Arts)
32 Avenue des Baumettes.
Tel: (93) 88 53 18.
Closed Mon and Oct.

**Musée International d'Art Naïf A.
Jakovsky,*
Château Ste Hélène,
Avenue Val-Maria.
Tel: (93) 71 78 33.
Closed Mon and some public holidays.

**Muséum d'Histoire Naturelle* (Musée
Barla),
60 Boulevard Risso.
Tel: (93) 55 15 24.
Closed Tues, Aug and some public
holidays.

**Musée de Malacologie,*
3 Cours Saleya.
Tel: (93) 85 18 44.
Closed Sun, Mon and some public
holidays.

**Galerie des Ponchettes,*
77 Quai des Etats Unis.
Tel: (93) 62 31 24.
Temporary exhibitions.

**Galerie d'Art Contemporain des Musées
de Nice,*
59 Quai des Etats Unis.
Tel: (93) 62 37 11.
Open: 2-7pm. Closed Mon, Oct and
some public holidays.
Temporary exhibitions.

*Galerie Municipale 'Renoir',
'Théâtre du Vieux Nice', Ilot des
Serruriers, Rue St Joseph.
Tel: (93) 80 58 37.
Open: May-Sept 4-8pm; Oct-Apr 3-5pm.
Closed Mon, Aug and some public
holidays.
Temporary exhibitions.

*Musée Naval,
Tour Bellanda, Parc du Château.
Closed Tues, some public holidays and
mid-Nov to mid-Dec.

*Galerie 'Nice-Etoile',
34 Avenue Jean Médecin.
Temporary exhibitions.

*Galerie 'Mossa',
Promenade du Paillon.
Temporary exhibitions.

*Centre Artistique,
Villa Arson, 20 Avenue Stéphen
Liégeard.
Tel: (93) 51 30 00.
Closed mid-July to Sept.
Temporary exhibitions.

*Couvent de Cimiez,
Nice-Cimiez.
Guided tours of special works of art at
10am, 11am, 3pm, 4pm, 5pm, 6pm,
except Sat pm, Sun and public holidays.

Musée National Marc Chagall,
Avenue Dr Ménard.
Tel: (93) 81 75 75.
Guided tours of 'Message Biblique'
available.
Open: July-Sept 10am-7pm; Oct-June
10am-12.30pm, 2-7.30pm. Closed Tues.
Free car park in basement.

Cathédrale Orthodoxe Russe,
Boulevard du Tsarevitch.
Guided tours available.
Closed am Sun.

Palais Lascaris,
15 Rue Droite.
Tel: (93) 62 05 54.
Open: daily except Mon July-Sept; Wed,
Thurs, Sat. Sun Oct-June.

Chapelle de la Miséricorde,
Place Pierre Gautier.
Apply to Office de Tourisme, 32 Rue de
l'Hotel-des-Postes.
Tel: (93) 85 25 25.

Musée du Vieux-Logis,
59 Avenue St Barthélemy.
Tel: (93) 84 44 74.
Open: 3-5pm Wed, Thurs, Sat and first
Sun of each month.

Terra Amata,
Musée de la Paléontologie Humaine,
25 Boulevard Carnot.
Tel: (93) 55 59 93.
Closed Mon.
Commentaries in English. Guided tours
available.

Musée Matisse & Musée Archéologique,
(including Roman baths, amphitheatre
and baptistry),
164 Avenue des Arènes-de-Cimiez, Nice-
Cimiez.
Tel: (93) 81 59 57.
Daily audio-visual performances.
Guided visits.
Closed am Sun, Mon and some public
holidays and Nov.

Nîmes
Single ticket gives entry to places
marked *.

*Arènes,
Boulevard Victor Hugo.

*Maison Carrée,
Boulevard Victor Hugo.

Jardin de la Fontaine & Temple de Diane,
Quai de la Fontaine.
Garden open during daylight hours.
Temple, like others with * open daily all
year.

Tour Magne,
Mont Cavalier.

*Musée d'Archéologie et d'Histoire
Naturelle,*
Boulevard Amiral Courbet.
Closed Sun.

Musée des Beaux-Arts,
Rue de la Cité-Foulc.
Closed Tues.

Musée de Vieux Nîmes,
in former episcopal palace near
cathedral.
Closed Sun.

Opio
Moulin d'Huile Roger Michel.
Closed Sun.

Orange
Théâtre Antique,
Place des Frères Mounet.
Open: all year; guided tours at 3.30pm
July to mid-Sept.

Musée Municipal,
almost opposite Théâtre Antique.
Same ticket valid for both. Open all
year.

Pernes-les-Fontaines
Tour Ferrande, Quai de Verdun.
Guided tour of frescoes at 5pm daily
except Sun and public holidays; 11am on
Sat.

Puyloubiers
Château dit du Général,
Musée de l'Institution des Invalides de la
Légion Etrangère.
Closed Mon.

Riez
Baptistry.
Keys at Office de Tourisme, Place des
Quinconces.
Tel: (92) 74 51 81.

Musée de la Nature en Provence,
Hôtel de Ville, 04500 Riez.
Tel: (92) 74 41 13.
Closed Sat. Geology, botany,
entomology.

Roquebrune-Cap Martin
Donjon (keep).
Closed Fri and Nov. Guided tours
available mid-July to Aug.

La Roque d'Antheron
Musée d'Archéologie Locale,
Place Paul Cézanne.
Tel: Office du Tourisme (42) 28 42 94.

St Chamas
Musée du Vieux St Chamas,
Montée des Pénitents.
Tel: (90) 50 90 54.

St Gilles
Eglise St Gilles.
Guided tours of crypt and Le Vis
staircase all year on the hour 9-11am, 3-
6pm, half-hourly July-Aug. Closed Jan-
Feb.

St Jean-Cap Ferrat
Musée Ile de France,
Fondation Ephrussi de Rothschild,
Boulevard Denis Séméria.
Tel: (93) 01 33 09.
Gardens open 9am-12 noon. Museum
open 3-7pm July and Aug; 2-6pm Sept-
June. Closed Mon and Nov.

Le Phare (lighthouse).
Open: am and pm all year.

St Maximin-la-Ste Baume
Basilique.
Open: am and pm daily.

St Michel-l'Observatoire
Observatoire de Haute Provence (2½km north on D305).
Open: Wed 3pm, and first Sun of each month 9.30am between Apr and Sept.
Guided tours of observatory available.

St Paul-de-Vence
Musée Municipal,
Rue Grande, above Syndicat d'Initiative.

Fondation Maeght (1km north-west).
Tel: (93) 32 81 63.
Open: am and pm all year, including gardens with statuary.

Musée Provençal,
Place de la Fontaine.
Closed Nov.

St Raphaël
Musée d'Archéologie Sous-Marine,
Rue des Templiers.
Closed Tues mid-June to mid-Sept; closed Sun mid-Sept to mid-June.

Musée du Vieux St Raphaël,
Eglise des Templiers, Rue des Templiers.
Same opening times as underwater archaeology museum next door.

St Rémy-de-Provence
St Paul-de-Mausole (1km south on D5).
Open: am and pm daily, but Vincent van Gogh's cell not open.

Musée Lapidaire,
Hôtel de Sade, Rue du Parège.
Guided tours June-Sept. Closed Tues; open weekends rest of year.

Musée des Alpilles Pierre de Brun,
Place Favier.

Roman triumphal arch and mausoleum,
2km south on right of D5.

Glanum archaeological site
(2km south on left of D5).
Tel: (90) 92 23 79.
Closed Tues Apr-Sept; closed Tues and Wed Oct-Mar.

St Tropez
Musée de l'Annonciade,
Place Georges Grammont.
Tel: (94) 97 04 01.
Closed Tues and Nov.

Citadelle & Musée de la Marine.
Closed Thurs and Nov.

Les Stes Maries-de-la-Mer
Crypt of church.
Open: am and pm Apr-Sept; all day Oct-Mar.

Musée Baroncelli,
Avenue Victor Hugo.
Closed Wed and Nov.

Salon-de-Provence
Musée de Salon et de la Crau,
Avenue de Pisair.
Open: 2-6pm weekdays; am and pm Sat, Sun and public holidays. Closed Tues.

Château de l'Empéri,
Musée National d'Art et d'Histoire Militaire.

Musée Nostradamus,
Boulevard Nostradamus.
Open: 2.30-6pm June-Oct, closed Tues.

Sanary-sur-Mer
Chapelle de Notre Dame de Beausset.
Open: 2-6pm from July to early Sept; 1.30-5pm Sun only early Sept to June.

Sault
Musée Municipal.
Open: 2-5pm from mid-June to mid-Sept. Closed Wed.

Saumane
Château des Marquis de Sade.
Open in summer.

Sénanque
Abbaye de Sénanque & Collections Sahariennes.
Tel: (90) 72 02 05.
Open: 10am-7pm June-Sept; 10am-12 noon, 2-6pm Oct-May. Guided tours available June-Sept.

Sérignan-du-Comtat
Musée Jean-Henri Fabre
(at edge of village on D976).
Tel: (90) 70 00 44.

La Seyne-sur-Mer
Musée Naval de la Seyne,
Fort de Balaguier, Corniche de Tamaris.
Tel: (94) 94 84 72.
Closed Mon and Tues.

Musée de la Mer.
Tel: (94) 94 88 67.
Closed Fri, am Sat, Mon.

Silvacane
Abbaye de Silvacane.
Closed Tues and Wed. Guided tours available.

Sisteron
La Citadelle & Musée de la Résistance.
Recorded commentary in French. Floodlit in summer.
Open all day. Closed mid-Nov to Apr.

Six-Fours-les-Plages
Ancienne Collégiale St Pierre
(at exit of Six-Fours on N559 towards Toulon, left on lane for 1½km).
Open: 2-5.30pm Sat and Sun.

Solliès-Ville
Maison Jean Aicard,
Local poet and novelist.
Closed Wed and Oct.

Taradeau
Musée Provençal,
Domaine de St Martin, 83460 Les Arcs.
Tel: (94) 73 02 01.
Local ethnography.

Tarascon
Château,
Boulevard du Château.
Guided tours all year at 10am, 11am, 2pm, 3pm, 4pm and at 9am and 5pm Apr-Sept. Closed Tues.

Abbaye St Michel-de-Frigolet
(8½km towards Avignon on N570, left on D81 for 3km).
Guided tours at intervals throughout day.

Le Thoronet
Abbaye du Thoronet
(4½km west on D79).
Guided tours available mid-July to Aug.

Toulon
Musée d'Art et d'Archéologie,
Boulevard du Maréchal Leclerc.
Tel: (94) 93 15 54.
Closed Mon and Thurs.

Musée Historique du Vieux Toulon,
Cours Lafayette.
Open: Mon, Wed, Sat pm only.

Musée Naval,
in Maritime Prefecture, Quai Stalingrad.

Tour Royale,
Pointe de la Mitre.
Tel: (94) 24 91 00.
Closed Mon and Nov-Feb. Guided tours only.

Muséum d'Histoire Naturelle,
20 Boulevard du Maréchal Leclerc.
Tel: (94) 93 15 54.
Open: am and pm all year.

Musée de la Mer,
69 Cours Lafayette.
Tel: (94) 24 42 97.

Mémorial National du Débarquement,
Tour Beaumont, Super-Toulon.
Open: am and pm all year.

La Turbie
Trophée des Alpes & museum.
Open: am and pm all year. Guided tours
available mid-July to mid-Sept.

Vaison-la-Romaine
Les Ruines Romaines & museum.
Open all day all year. Guided tours
available July-Sept.

Vallauris
Musée National Picasso.
Open all day all year.

Musée Municipal,
Château de Vallauris, Place de la
Libération.
Tel: (93) 64 16 05.
Permanent exhibition of ceramics. Open
daily all year.

Galerie Madoura.
Ceramics workshop.
Closed Sat and Sun.

Valréas
Hôtel de Ville,
Place Aristide Briand.
Old Hôtel de Simiane (part Gothic and
early eighteenth-century).
Open: am and pm.

Chapelle des Pénitents Blancs,
Place Pie.
Open: July to mid-Sept am and pm.

Venasque
Baptistère.
Closed 12 noon-2pm.

Vence
Chapelle du Rosaire (Chapelle Matisse),
Route de St Jeannet.
Tel: (93) 58 03 26.
Open: Tues and Thurs 10-11.30am, 2.30-
5.30pm, or by special arrangement.

Vernègues
Château-Bas (2km south on D22 and left
for 2km).
Ruins of Roman temple in grounds.
Serious students may apply to keeper in
main building.

La Verdière
Château.
Open: am and pm all year.

Villefranche-sur-Mer
Chapelle St Pierre,
Port des Pêcheurs.
Guided tours available to fishermen's
chapel decorated by Jean Cocteau.
Closed Fri and mid-Nov to mid-Dec.

Centre de Documentation et Animation,
Citadelle.
Tel: (93) 55 45 12.
Temporary exhibitions for school and
adult parties.

Musée Volti.
Sculptures.
Closed Nov.

Villeneuve-lès-Avignon
Tour Philippe-le-Bel,
Avenue Gabriel Péri.
Closed Tues and Feb.

Fort St André,
Rue Montée du Fort St André.

Chartreuse du Val de Bénédiction,
Rue de la République.

Musée Municipal,
Rue de l'Hôpital.
Closed Tues and Feb.

Villeneuve-Loubet
Musée d'Art Culinaire (Fondation
Auguste Escoffier),
Place de la Mairie.
Closed Mar and Nov.

Visan
Notre Dame des Vignes
(1km south-east off D20).
Open: 9am-12 noon, 3-7pm in summer.
Closed Sun am and Thurs.

COUNTRY INNS

The small rural inns given below are a
personal selection from among the many
in the region. They are listed under the
départements including that segment of
Drôme which abuts Vaucluse. Each
hotel has some quality which helps to
make a holiday memorable, whether for
comfort, warmth of welcome, food, the
attractiveness of the building or its
setting. The inclusion of a hotel in this
list is not an automatic guarantee of its
excellence; ownership, staff and
circumstances can change abruptly.
 The name of the hotel is followed by
(1), (2) or (3), rough price-guides to full-
or half-board, from simple and relatively
inexpensive (1), through medium (2) to
fairly expensive (3) in this range of
hotels, though not necessarily when
compared with similar hotels in coastal
resorts and large tourist centres. The
hotels are likely to appear in the current
year's edition of *Guide Michelin* or *Guide
des Logis de France,* both invaluable for
touring in France.
 When booking ahead by post write in
French and enclose an International
Reply Coupon (sold at Post Offices).
Confirmation of a booking may be
accompanied by a request for a deposit
(*arrhes*). This can be paid through a
bank, National Girobank, or by a
personal cheque made out in francs for
the amount demanded. This sum will be
deducted from the total bill.

Alpes-de-Haute Provence

Avenue (1),
04240 Annot.
Tel: (92) 83 22 07.

Le Relais du Lac (1),
04340 Le Lauzet.
Tel: (92) 85 51 07.

St Clair (1),
04230 St Etienne-les-Orgues (2km
south).
Tel: (92) 76 07 09.

Alpes-Maritimes

Horizon (1),
Cabris, 06530 Peymeinade.
Tel: (93) 60 51 69.

Hostellerie Lou Castellet (1),
06510 Carros (4km south-east).
Tel: (93) 29 16 66.

Val Casterino (1),
Casterino, 06430 Tende.
Tel: (93) 04 64 38.

Le Petite Auberge (2),
Coaraze, 06390 Contes.
Tel: (93) 79 01 69.

La Méditerranée (1),
06440 Lucéram.
Tel: (93) 91 54 54.

Pierrot-Pierrette (2),
Monti, 06500 Menton.
Tel: (93) 35 79 76.

Auberge de la Madone (3),
Peillon, 06440 L'Escarène.
Tel: (93) 91 91 17.

Terminus (1),
St Dalmas-de-Tende, 06430 Tende (4km
south-east).
Tel: (93) 04 60 10.

Auberge Bon Puits (2),
Le Suquet, 06450 Lantosque.
Tel: (93) 03 17 65.

Bouches-du-Rhône

La Benvengudo (3),
Les Baux-de-Provence, 13520
Maussane-les-Alpilles.
Tel: (90) 97 32 50.

Relais Ste-Victoire (2),
Beaurecueil, 13100 Aix-en-Provence.
Tel: (42) 28 94 34.

Le Réal (2),
13490 Jouques.
Tel: (42) 57 81 05.

L'Oustaloun (2),
13520 Maussane-les-Alpilles.
Tel: (90) 97 32 19.

Drôme

Auberge du Vieux Village (3),
Aubres, 26110 Nyons.
Tel: (75) 26 12 89.

Les Oliviers (2),
26170 Buis-les-Baronnies.
Tel: (75) 26 08 77.

Le Mirabeau (1),
Mirabel-aux-Baronnies, 26110 Nyons.
Tel: (75) 27 11 47.

Le Dauphin (1),
Montségur-sur-Lauzon, 26130 St Paul-
Trois-Châteaux.
Tel: (75) 98 11 56.

Dauphiné-Provence (1),
Sahune, 26510 Rémuzat.
Tel: (75) 26 35 99.

Auberge des Quatre Saisons (3),
St Restitut, 26130 St Paul-Trois-
Châteaux.
Tel: (75) 04 71 88.

Ferme St Michel (2),
Solérieux, 26130 St Paul-Trois-
Châteaux.
Tel: (75) 98 10 66.

Var

Les Palmiers (3)
Cabasson, 83230 Bormes-les-Mimosas.
Tel: (94) 64 80 00.

Mas du Four (2),
Le Cannet-des-Maures, 83340 Le Luc
(2½km east).
Tel: (94) 60 74 64.

Grand Hôtel Bain (1),
83840 Comps-sur-Artuby.
Tel: (94) 76 90 06.

Auberge du Vieux Fox (3),
Fox-Amphoux, 83670 Barjols.
Tel: (94) 80 71 69.

Bello Visto (3),
Gassin, 83990 St Tropez.
Tel: (94) 56 17 30.

Coteau Fleuri (2),
83360 Grimaud.
Tel: (94) 43 20 17.

Parc (1),
83510 Lorgues.
Tel: (94) 73 70 01.

Deux Rocs (3),
Seillans, 83440 Fayence.
Tel: (94) 76 05 33.

Vaucluse

Relais du Ventoux (1),
Aurel, 84390 Sault.
Tel: (90) 64 00 62.

Les Geraniums (1),
Le Barroux, 84330 Caromb.
Tel: (90) 62 41 08.

L'Aiguebrun (3),
84480 Bonnieux, (6km south-east).
Tel: (90) 74 04 14.

Aux Ombrelles (1),
84160 Cadenet.
Tel: (90) 68 02 40.

Le Beffroi (3),
84330 Caromb.
Tel: (90) 62 45 63.

L'Etang (2),
Cucuron, 84160 Cadenet.
Tel: (90) 77 21 25.

Les Florets (2),
Gigondas, 84190 Beaumes-de-Venise.
Tel: (90) 65 85 01.

Hostellerie des Commandeurs (1),
Joucas, 84220 Gordes.
Tel: (90) 72 00 05.

La Chaumière (2),
84360 Lauris.
Tel: (90) 68 01 29.

Auberge de Rustreou (2),
Rustrel, 84400 Apt.
Tel: (90) 74 24 12.

Voyageurs (2),
84490 St Saturnin-d'Apt.
Tel: (90) 75 42 08.

La Table du Comtat (3),
Seguret, 84110 Vaison-la-Romaine.
Tel: (90) 36 91 49.

BIBLIOGRAPHY

Ardagh, John, *The South of France.*
(Mitchell Beazley, 1983.) Compact,
informative, readable introduction and
gazetteer.
Brangham, A.N., *The Naturalist's
Riviera.* (Phoenix House, 1962.) Flora
and fauna in relation to climate and
environment.
Brangham, A.N., *Provence.* (Spurbooks,
1976.) Impressions of landscapes, places
and history.
Cameron, Roderick, *The Golden Riviera.*
(Weidenfeld & Nicolson, 1975.) History,
description, reminiscence by a resident.
Dix, Carol, *The Camargue.* (Gollancz,
1975.) Survey of life, nature, traditions
and history.
Higham, Roger, *Provençal Sunshine.*
(Dent, 1969.) A spring tour on foot.
Howarth, Patrick, *When the Riviera was
Ours.* (Routledge & Kegan Paul, 1977.)
Social and literary history.
Lyall, Archibald, *The Companion Guide
to the South of France* (revised A.N.
Brangham). (Collins, 1978.) Art and
architectural sites, history.
Michelin Green Guide, *Provence*
(current English edition). General
introduction and gazetteer for Western
Provence.
Michelin Green Guide, *French Riviera,
Côte d'Azur* (current English edition).
Eastern Provence and Alpes-Maritimes.
Moyal, Maurice, *On the Road to Pastures
New.* (Phoenix House, 1956.) First-hand
description of seasonal migration of
sheep.
Pope-Hennessy, James, *Aspects of
Provence.* (Longmans, 1952.) Elegantly
written evocation.
Turnbull, Patrick, *Provence.* (Batsford,
1972.) Informative, diverting by one
who has lived there.
Weber, Karl & Hoffmann, Lukas,
Camargue. (Harrap, 1970.) Sumptuous
illustrations and authoritative text about
wildlife.
Whelpton, Barbara, *Painter's Provence.*
(Johnson, 1970.) Brief guide to some
artists, museums, architecture and
archaeology.

Index

(Figures in italics refer to illustrations)

157